A personal journey into the mystery of the Shroud

Dedication

To the Way, The truth and the Life

John 14:6

© SLT 2025

A personal journey into the mystery of the Shroud

Table of Contents

Chapter 1: The Calling 4

Chapter 2: A New Enigma 8

Chapter 3: The Carbon Dating of the Cloth 26
    A reexamination of the data uncovered several critical statistical flaws that
    erode confidence: 30
    Technology Evolves 31

Chapter 4: The Image 33
    The Study of the Image Goes High-Tech 38

Chapter 5: The STURP Team Scientific Disciplines 44
    Notable STURP Team Members included: 45
    Directional Radiation Hypothesis 46
    Types of Radiation and Experimental Support 46
    Implications and Scientific Summary 47
    Key Findings of the STURP Study 48
    The STURP final report concluded: 53
    Vapors or Gases from Body Fluids 55
    Decomposition Products and Chemical Reactions 56
    Direct Contact or Fluid Transfer 56
    Timing and Condition 57
    The STURP team in their analysis: 57
    Radiation Theory 61
    Creation a superficial, Shroud-like image with radiation 63
    Terms in plain language 63
    Radiation-Based Methods for Superficial Image Creation: Expanded
    Explanation 64

    Challenges of Distance and Timing: 65
    The event horizon theory: 66

Chapter 6: Artificial Intelligence 71
    Enhanced Image Analysis and Pattern Recognition 73
    Material and Chemical Composition Analysis 73
    Carbon Dating and Chronology Verification 73
    Reconstruction of Historical Context 74
    Simulation of Image Formation Mechanisms 74
    Preservation and Authentication Methods 74

Chapter 7: Who is it? 77

Chapter 8: How and why was it done? 82

Chapter 9: Technology Advances 91
    Moving forward again: 92
    We look to Artificial Intelligence (AI) 97
    Hidden Geometric Patterns: 97
    Image Formation Radiation or an Intense Energy Burst 101
    Hidden Patterns and 3D Properties Revealed 101

Chapter 10: My conclusions 104
    The Provenance 105
    The Carbon 14 dating 108
    The Image: 111
    What is the image and how was it formed? 114
    Religious Breakdown of the STURP Team 117

Chapter 11: The Shroud as a Time Capsule 131
    Science reaches Its limits 132

Chapter 1: The Calling

My Wall Street career centered on synthesizing diverse perspectives and concrete data to uncover subtle strategies for gaining a competitive edge in a sea of professional investors. This involved not just crunching numbers but weaving together threads from economics, geopolitics, and even environmental factors to forecast shifts that others overlooked. I honed the ability to identify correlations between seemingly unrelated factors to predict market trends, a skill that demanded both intuition and rigorous analysis. A straightforward example is how an oil discovery in a remote region could increase global supply, lower oil prices, and boost airline stocks due to their heavy reliance on fuel, illustrating how a single event ripples through interconnected sectors. A more complex case emerged when I was tasked with analyzing mortgage-backed securities and the decision-making processes behind their trading. These intricate securities pool mortgages into a single investment vehicle, balancing diversified risk with investor returns, a delicate equilibrium critical to housing market liquidity and broader economic stability. Disruptions to this balance, as seen in the 2008 financial crisis, can precipitate catastrophic consequences underscoring the fragility of financial systems built on such instruments. While scrutinizing these securities I uncovered a compelling insight that transformed our trading approach. Regulatory guidelines dictated mortgage securities structure, including factors, like mortgage maturity, location, and interest rates, which influence their performance in unpredictable ways. Although geographic diversity was a stated objective to mitigate risks it was often loosely applied in practice, leaving vulnerabilities exposed. By examining external factors impacting mortgages such as unemployment spikes or natural disasters, I noted that hurricanes frequently triggered insurance-driven mortgage prepayments. These events could cascade through the market. Triggering prepayments injecting significant cash into mortgage-backed securities, rapidly altering their value and creating opportunities for savvy investors. I developed a system that weighted securities by geographic composition and integrated hurricane prediction models, enabling traders to identify positions likely to experience value shifts as storms approached. Creating a predictive tool that anticipated real-world disruptions with remarkable accuracy. This innovation delivered substantial profits for the trading desk. Proving the value of interdisciplinary analysis in finance, by combining data on weather, geography, and mortgages.

I achieved an unexpected breakthrough that highlighted the power of connecting disparate data points. This analytical approach, blending quantitative rigor with qualitative insights, set me on a path toward a discovery that would profoundly transform my life, bridging my professional expertise with personal explorations of history and mystery.

Years later, after leaving Wall Street, I found myself captivated by a Western movie suggesting that the notorious outlaw Billy the Kid was not killed by Pat Garrett but lived a long life under a different identity. A narrative that sparked my curiosity about historical truths hidden beneath popular myths. Intrigued, I delved into the story's basis in fact, questioning the official accounts that had shaped American folklore. I discovered that in 1950, a man claiming to be Billy the Kid petitioned the Governor of New Mexico for a pardon promised by Governor Wallace in the 1800s, a bold claim that invited scrutiny of long-buried records. I meticulously studied seven books, prioritizing those with firsthand accounts from individuals who had met William Bonney, seeking insights into his personality, mannerisms, and background to test the claimant's veracity. Using the same cross-referential analysis I employed in finance, comparing known facts, personality traits, and historical circumstances against timelines and motivations. I evaluated the claims with a critical eye. surprisingly, the sequence of events aligned more closely with the claimant evidence than many historical accounts, revealing inconsistencies in the traditional narrative that suggested deeper layers to the story. The detailed findings warrant a separate book, but I concluded that history is not always as it seems, often shaped by incomplete records or biased re-tellings. In the absence of definitive evidence historians often rely on conjecture. Conjecture can be influenced by political, social, or financial motives. Actual truth can be obscured by the agendas of those who record it. Extraordinary claims require extraordinary evidence, a scientific principle that poses a significant hurdle for many mysteries, demanding rigorous verification before acceptance. However, I also adhere to Occam's Razor, which posits that the simplest explanation is often the most likely, favoring hypotheses that introduce the fewest assumptions. For further details on who Garrett may have killed, or who William Bonney truly was, and what became of him. I recommend Daniel A. Edwards' well-researched book, Billy the Kid: An Autobiography, which provides a compelling case grounded in primary sources and logical deduction.

However, when I shared my excitement with family and friends, their reactions were lukewarm, akin to watching ice melt slowly under a dim light, offering polite interest but little enthusiasm. My wife remarked, "That's interesting, but who cares about Billy the Kid? You need to find a more significant project," her words gently nudging me toward pursuits with broader impact. Though the actual pursuit was personally rewarding, providing intellectual stimulation and a sense of uncovering hidden truths. I recognized that it carried only niche appeal. A potential for contentious debate tied to political and economic implications, limiting its resonance with a wider audience. It was time to move on, seeking a mystery of greater historical weight that could engage both my analytical skills and a sense of universal intrigue. Turning to my laptop, I searched Google for the most investigated artifact in the world. Very curious as to what enigma had captured the collective imagination of scholars and scientists alike. The answer surprised me:The Shroud of Turin, an object that promised to blend history, science, and profound questions about faith in ways my financial background had never anticipated.

Chapter 2: A New Enigma

In 1988, a newspaper article dismissing the Shroud of Turin, as a medieval forgery, first caught my attention. The bold headline challenging long-held beliefs about this enigmatic cloth. The piece cited a carbon-dating study conducted by the University of Arizona, Oxford University, and the Federal Institute of Technology in Zurich, which placed the cloth's origin between 1260 and 1390 AD, centuries removed from the time of Christ, casting doubt on its biblical connections. As a Roman Catholic I was educated in Catholic institutions through my undergraduate years, where faith was woven into daily life. Later I studied at a secular university, while earning my MBA, where skepticism was encouraged. I approached the mystery with both curiosity and caution, balancing inherited beliefs with a demand for empirical evidence. Determined to set aside religious preconceptions that might cloud judgment, I grounded my inquiry in science and history, adopting a rigorously secular, evidence-based perspective that prioritized facts over faith. Basically, a common-sense approach that sought truth through verifiable data rather than assumption.

A common-sense approach to the provenance of the Shroud of Turin involves starting with an objective reading of the Shroud itself, carefully examining its physical features and comparing them with historical and biblical data about Jesus' passion and burial, identifying alignments or discrepancies. This entails tracing the Shroud's documented history from its first appearances in records. Evaluating scientific examinations like radiocarbon dating and considering the broader medieval context of relic production, pilgrimages that often-blurred lines between authentic artifacts and pious forgeries. Scholars typically place the Shroud's origin in the 14th century, consistent with when it first appeared in historical records, and view many claims about its authenticity as influenced by confirmation bias rather than solid verification, where believers see what they wish to see. Scientific analyses have suggested medieval manufacturing techniques or art methods that could explain the image, such as pigment applications or bas-relief rubbings. Historical and archaeological evidence supports skepticism about it being the actual burial cloth of Jesus, given the gaps in early custody. Thus, the common-sense approach balances assessed scientific, historical, and textual evidence with an awareness of psychological biases that can skew interpretation. Which results in a cautious stance on authenticity that avoids dogmatic conclusions. Flavored with my own brand of weighing correlating information that includes standard scholarly consensus, and a healthy dose of Bayesian Probability. This method allows for open- minded exploration while anchoring in established knowledge. Bayesian probability is an interpretation of probability that represents a degree of belief or knowledge about an event or hypothesis, rather than frequency or propensity. It allows for the updating of this belief based on new evidence using Bayes' theorem. This means it calculates the probability of a hypothesis being true by combining prior knowledge (prior probability) with new data (likelihood), resulting in an updated probability (posterior probability).

A key concept of Bayesian probability is an interpretation of probability that represents a state of knowledge or a degree of belief in a hypothesis, rather than a long-run frequency of events. It quantifies how strongly one believes in an event or hypothesis given prior information. Then it updates this belief as new evidence becomes available. Bayesian probability is widely used in situations where knowledge evolves over time, such as in medical diagnosis, robotics, and decision-making under uncertainty.

However, what began as a skeptical investigation, driven by a search for an unresolved mystery, soon evolved into a journey that would profoundly reshape my understanding of truths I had once taken for granted. Revealing layers of complexity that defied simple dismissal. I was pulled into an experience that I was unprepared for nor did I expect. My objective was not to create new research but to use the existing work to come to a personal conclusion.

My first step was to trace the Shroud of Turin's provenance and scrutinize the 1988 carbon-dating study in depth, examining methodologies and potential flaws to assess its reliability. Whether regarded as an icon of devotion or a relic of history, the Shroud's historical and cultural significance endures continuing to influence art, theology, and science across centuries. I was intrigued, however, by why it continues to captivate scientists even after being labeled a medieval artifact by the 1988 carbon dating, a verdict that should have ended debate but instead ignited more questions. Initially more than 60 researchers from fields as diverse as chemistry, biology, medical forensics, optical image analysis, textile analysis, physics, archeology, palynology, hematology, radiocarbon dating, microscopy, materials science, photography, image processing, art history, and computer science have studied it. They continue to study it in increasing numbers, drawn by anomalies that challenge conventional explanations. This unparalleled interdisciplinary effort, spanning decades and disciplines, underscores why the Shroud remains the world's most studied artifact, a testament to its enduring puzzle. My goal was not to replicate this work but to synthesize its findings into a coherent narrative that I can appreciate and understand, making the complex accessible through logical connections.

Guided by the principle that extraordinary claims require extraordinary evidence, a cornerstone of scientific inquiry that demands robust proof for bold assertions. I sought to determine whether the Shroud's claim as Jesus' burial cloth obscured its true nature as a medieval creation or revealed something deeper about its origins and purpose. If the Shroud is Jesus' burial cloth, its lineage would begin in the first century, as referenced in the New Testament accounts of the crucifixion and entombment it provides a direct link to biblical events. If not, its story would start around 1260 AD, consistent with the carbon-dating results and aligning with the rise of relic veneration in medieval Europe. The Gospels mention a linen cloth used to wrap Jesus's body, sindon (fine linen) in Mark 15:46 and othonia (linen wrappings) in Luke 24:12 and John 20:5–7, with John noting a separate cloth, the sudarium, covering the face to honor Jewish customs. Notably, nowhere in the Gospels is an image described as forming on the Shroud, a detail that raises questions about how such a feature could emerge if tied to the passion narrative. This discrepancy is a point of serious contention for an icon (or relic) purported to carry a miraculous full-body image, suggesting that any imprint might stem from later traditions rather than scriptural description.

An image, that is linked to Catholic tradition rather than the Gospel narratives directly is the Veil of Veronica. According to Christian tradition, a woman named Veronica met Jesus on the road to Calvary. She offered him her veil to wipe his face, and miraculously, his image was imprinted on the cloth. This story is not found in the canonical Gospels; it first appears in later apocryphal writings and devotional traditions (around the 11th century). By the late Middle Ages, multiple churches across Europe claimed to possess the "true" veil (such as in Jaén, Spain; Manoppello, Italy; and Compiègne, France). The Manoppello Veil (kept in the Sanctuary of the Holy Face in Abruzzo, Italy) is one of the most famous claimants today. Some modern researchers even propose that this transparent cloth could be the original "Veronica's Veil". especially Father Heinrich Pfeiffer of the Pontifical Gregorian University, believe to be the authentic Veil of Veronica. Pfeiffer announced his conviction after years of study, but the Vatican has not officially supported this claim, and some scholars remain skeptical. Traditionally, the relic known as the Veil of Veronica is said to be preserved within St. Peter's Basilica in Rome, where it is displayed during special ceremonies, and is referenced in the liturgy and church traditions. The Vatican continues to venerate a cloth believed to be Veronica's Veil, though its authenticity is debated, and no definitive scientific verification has resolved competing claims.

Numerous copies and images claimed to have touched or to relate to the original Veil have circulated over centuries, and shrines sometimes display these as part of devotional practice. The League of St. Martin has facilitated distribution of such copies recently, citing their contact with the revered Vatican relic. Many historians and theologians consider the story of Veronica's Veil to be legendary, with its origins in medieval tradition and the name "Veronica" itself symbolizing "true image." There is little direct historical evidence for the existence or miraculous properties of the cloth, and no uncontested physical or documentary chain of custody.

The origin and development of the Stations of the Cross (Via Crucis) are rooted in early Christian practice and the longing of pilgrims to retrace Jesus's path to crucifixion, fostering a tangible connection to the events of the Passion. After Christianity was legalized in the Roman Empire in the 4th century and the Church of the Holy Sepulcher was established in Jerusalem, pilgrims began tracing Jesus's Passion during Holy Week, turning devotion into a physical journey. The earliest written account of these processions comes from the 4th-century pilgrim Egeria, whose writings preserved this devotional practice, describing rituals that brought the biblical story to life. By the 5th century, European churches began replicating Jerusalem's key sites for those unable to travel, adapting the experience to local contexts. For example, the monastery of San Stefano in Bologna constructed chapels representing moments from the Passion, allowing devotees to participate without leaving home. The term "Stations": The word "stations," in this context, appears first in the 15th century, when English pilgrim William Wey described the customary halting points along the Via Sacra in Jerusalem, marking pauses for prayer and reflection. Pilgrims would retrace Christ's steps in either direction, adapting to circumstances. Political instability and travel difficulties to Jerusalem helped the practice spread widely throughout Europe during the Middle Ages, varying in number and form to suit different communities. From the 14th century onward, Franciscans became custodians of holy sites in Jerusalem, promoting and standardizing the devotion with structured guides. In 1686, Pope Innocent XI allowed Franciscans to erect Stations in their churches and granted indulgences to participants, encouraging widespread adoption; this was extended to all churches in 1731 by Pope Clement XII, who fixed the number at 14 stations for uniformity. Today, the Stations of the Cross are set at 14 stations, commemorating key events from Jesus's condemnation to his burial, each inviting meditation on suffering and redemption. They remain a central component of Catholic devotional life, especially during Lent, blending history, prayer, and empathy. Veronica's veil having any reference to the Shroud is pure speculation, a legendary element without direct ties, yet the image left on a cloth does create wonder if it is purely coincidental or part of a larger pattern of miraculous imprints in Christian lore.

This is the image on the Veil of Veronica held in the village of Manoppello.

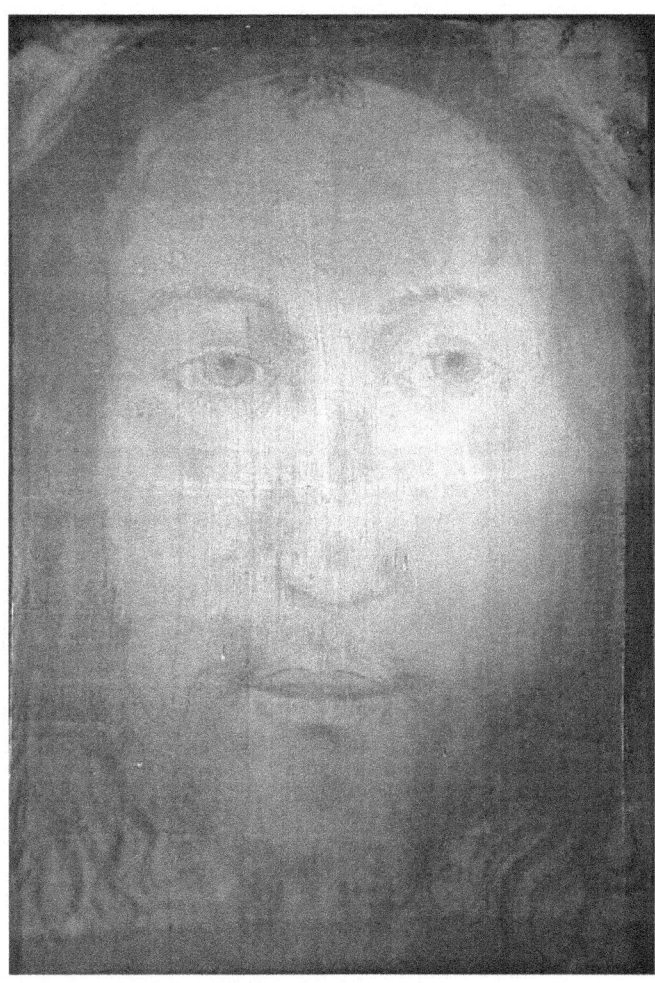

A personal journey into the mystery of the Shroud

This is the AI enhancement of the image on the Veil of Veronica held in the village of Manoppello.

This is the AI enhanced image from the Shroud of Turin.

Interesting, how similar AI depicts the two images. Which is the actual face of Jesus? The Veil has no biblical reference.

The placement of the Shroud over the Body.

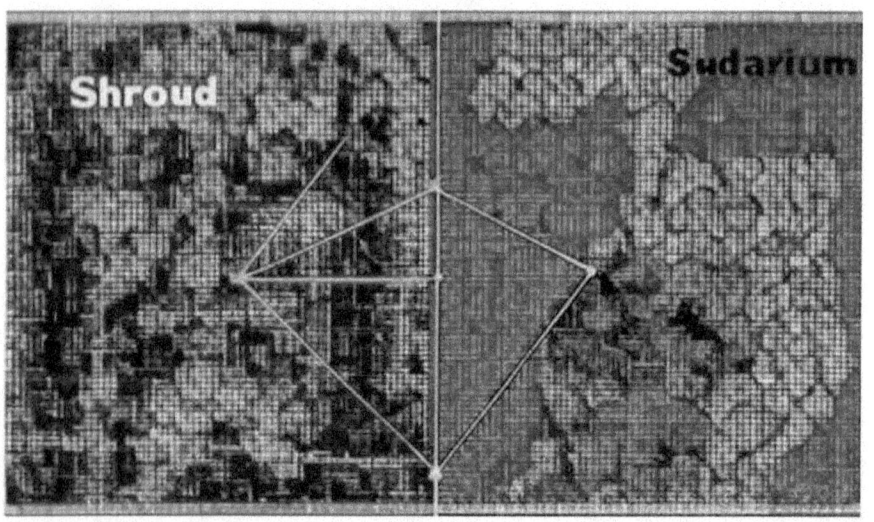

Shroud   Sudarium

Note: The blood stains on the Sudarium line up with the face on the Shroud.

A related relic, the Sudarium of Oviedo, dated to Jerusalem before 614 AD., offers a comparative anchor that strengthens arguments for ancient origins. Historical records indicate it was removed from

Jerusalem during the 614 AD Persian invasion, a chaotic event that scattered sacred objects, traveling through Alexandria and North Africa before reaching Spain. I Spain it found sanctuary housed in Oviedo's Cathedral of San Salvador. We can see in the above illustration when digitized and overlayed on the Shroud the Sudarium's bloodstains and blood type align with the Shroud's. This provides a forensic link that challenges the 1988 dating and suggests shared provenance. The Shroud's early history is less clear and riddled with large gaps that invite speculation, yet patterns emerge upon closer examination. In the 4th century, Eusebius of Caesarea documented a legendary exchange between King Abgar V of Edessa and Jesus linked to the Image of Edessa or Mandylion, a cloth bearing Jesus's face that became a focal point of early Christian veneration. Early tradition says an image of Christ's face (the Image of Edessa/Mandylion) was kept at Edessa from late antiquity and revered as a divine gift. A prominent hypothesis (Ian Wilson and others) is that the Mandylion was the Shroud, folded so only the face showed ("tetrapylon"), which would explain later descriptions of a facial image without a full body. This is debated but has garnered sustained scholarly attention and fits later evidence, bridging gaps in the chain of custody. After Abgar's death in 50 AD, his son Manu VI, who rejected Christianity, prompted a bishop to hide the cloth in a tunnel wall in Edessa, where it remained for centuries, protected from persecution. Critics note this gap in the record and the lack of evidence that this cloth is the Shroud, highlights the challenges of tracing artifacts through turbulent times. However, intriguing clues emerge that build a circumstantial case. Around 525 AD, a flood in Edessa led to the cloth's rediscovery during reconstruction efforts, bringing it back into the light. By 550 AD, Christian art began depicting a bearded face resembling the

Shroud's image, a shift that coincides with the relic's influence on iconography. Monks Theodosius and Isadore, custodians of the Edessa image, spread its likeness across the region, disseminating copies that preserved its essence. Circumstantial evidence, at best, but still coinciding with the change in the image of the face of Jesus, suggesting cultural transmission. The Image of Edessa was brought with imperial ceremony to Constantinople in August 944 and commemorated annually (Feast of the Mandylion), elevating its status. If the Mandylion equals the folded Shroud, then the Shroud reached Constantinople in 944 where it remained for 260 years, integrated into Byzantine religious life. Multiple Byzantine references and later art point to a revered cloth bearing Christ's image present in the capital after 944; proponents argue some details (full-length body hints, "imprinted" image language) align better with the Shroud than with a painted icon, offering a nuanced fit. The identification isn't unanimous but, this is the strongest single staging point before the West, providing a pivotal link. When Crusaders sacked the city in 1204, many relics moved West amid the chaos, dispersing treasures. There's no surviving official inventory explicitly naming "a Shroud of Christ," but a number of scholars argue that an image/cloth matching later descriptions likely left the imperial Pharos Chapel with other Passion relics, inferred from patterns of relocation. That "gap" (no clear label saying "this is the Shroud") is the main weakness in the chain, yet it mirrors the elusive nature of many ancient artifacts.

Louis IX famously centralized Passion relics at the Sainte-Chapelle in Paris, creating a grand repository. Detailed work on its inventories suggests a "Holy Cloth/Holy Face" reliquary (dimensions large enough for a folded long cloth) that later disappears from the records before the 1530s—right when the Shroud appears in France (Lirey, 1350s), timing that invites connection. Several sindonologists argue this is the most plausible pipeline to Lirey, tracing a path through royal collections. It's circumstantial but comparatively robust among the hypotheses, supported by archival hints. Another live option is a private transfer from the East into the hands of Geoffroy de Charny (the Shroud's first known owner) or his circle, sometimes, linked to campaigns like Smyrna (1346) or to Templar custody after 1204, Templar knights who guarded sacred items. There's no smoking-gun document naming the Shroud, but de Charny's possession by c. 1355 is certain and documented in church records. In 1204, French knight Robert de Clari documented seeing the Shroud in Constantinople before it vanished during the Fourth Crusade's looting, an eyewitness account adding credibility. Speculative links tie it to the Knights Templar and Geoffroi de Charny, who possessed it in Lirey, France by the mid-14th century, possibly acquired through military exploits. To ease East-West religious tensions, the Pope reportedly commissioned a front-side-only painted duplicate and imposed an edict of silence on de Charny, ensuring the original's protection. In 1389, Bishop Pierre d'Arcis of Troyes objected to its display, citing a supposed artist's confession of forgery. A claim possibly driven by political motives to control relic traffic. After de Charny's death, the Shroud passed to the de Vergy family, who held it until 1389, when papal permission allowed public exhibitions in Chambéry, France, starting in 1502, marking its transition to wider veneration.

From Lirey exhibitions (1350s) to the Savoy acquisition (1453), then to Chambery (fire in 1532) and finally Turin in 1578, is the firm Shroud part of the chain well-documented and unbroken, providing a solid foundation for later history. A 1532 fire at Chambéry's Sainte-Chapelle damaged the Shroud, with molten silver leaving scorch marks and holes that threatened its integrity. The Poor Clare nuns repaired the Shroud in 1534 using a French invisible weave technique, reinforcing damaged areas with linen triangles backed by Holland cloth, a meticulous restoration. The repairs were so precise that 20th-century microscopy initially missed them, demonstrating the skill involved. In 1578, the Shroud was moved to Turin Italy, where it remains, safeguarded in the Cathedral of St. John the Baptist. The Shroud is a herringbone weave linen consistent with burial cloths for affluent individuals in the 1st century, a luxury material befitting Joseph of Arimathea's status.

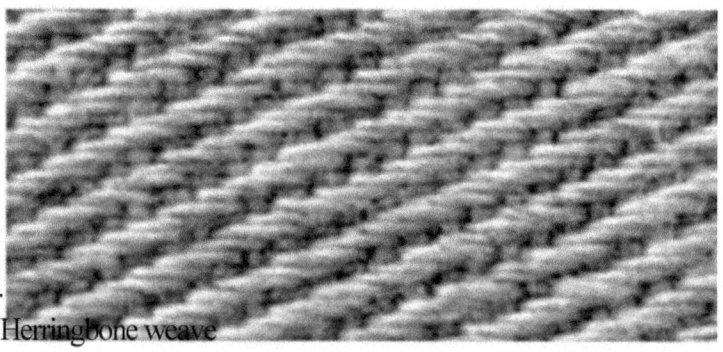
Herringbone weave

The Gospels describe Jesus's burial by Joseph of Arimathea, a wealthy Sanhedrin member, making such a cloth plausible for a respectful entombment. Jerusalem-specific pollen and soil traces further suggest a Middle Eastern origin, unlikely for a European forgery, as these elements point to the Holy Land. Four of the plant species discovered were selected as geographic indicators, because their distribution is restricted to the Middle East, narrowing the possible location. The area where their boundaries overlap is a narrow strip of land between Jerusalem and Hebron, a precise correlation. Only in this area could people bring fresh plants of these species and lay them on the body of a dead man, aligning with burial practices.

Eight of the blooming plant species found inside the Shroud share a common blooming time of March-April, matching the timing of Passover and crucifixion. Pollen is found in dust particles throughout the entire Shroud of Turin, not in specific localized areas, with studies suggesting the presence of plants indigenous to Israel, Turkey, Middle East, and Europe. Key pollen species like Gundelia turneries point to a strong connection with Jerusalem and the surrounding regions. The distribution of pollen suggests the cloth spent time in Jerusalem, later moving to Edessa (Turkey) and then Constantinople before arriving in Europe.

The Sudarium's matching bloodstains and earlier provenance bolster this case for authenticity, offering complementary evidence. However, the 1988 carbon-dating results (1260–1390 AD) fuel skepticism among critics. Shroud believers argue the tested samples may have been contaminated or taken from repaired sections, invalidating the medieval verdict. Forensic scientist Walter McCrone's findings of red ochre and vermilion pigments on the Shroud contributed to forgery claims. The phrase "vermilion on the Shroud" refers to the presence of vermilion, a bright red pigment made from mercury sulfide, on the Shroud of Turin. Scientific analysis, particularly by microscopist Walter McCrone, found that what appeared to be bloodstains were actually painted with vermilion pigment in a gelatin medium, rather than being genuine blood, a discovery that swayed opinions toward artistic creation. Vermilion, along with red ochre, was a common pigment used by artists during the Middle Ages, supporting the argument that the Shroud is a medieval creation rather than an authentic relic from antiquity, as it mimicked blood for dramatic effect. The presence of vermilion is significant because it is not a component of natural blood but an artist's pigment, suggesting that the red marks were added to simulate blood and enhance the visual impact of the image, a technique common in devotional art. This finding is a key issue in the debate about the authenticity of the Shroud of Turin, pointing to human craftsmanship. It leads to the identification of artistic pigments like vermilion as strong evidence that the Shroud was created as an artistic or devotional object rather than being an actual burial cloth from the time of Jesus. Although there is minimal support for claims, findings could relate to the papal duplicate, a painted copy. The duplicate was said to have been placed on the original after completion as a "Blessing" for the duplicate, potentially transferring trace pigments. Later findings show that the amount of vermilion on the Shroud was minuscule, supporting a touching of a duplicate not original painting, thus not contaminating the primary image.

The Shroud's unique characteristics, its weave, pollen, and Sudarium correlations, continue to challenge the medieval dating creating a tension between evidence streams. The Shroud of Turin intertwines history, science, and faith in a tapestry that defies easy resolution. While no definitive chain of custody proves it is Jesus' burial cloth, circumstantial evidence like pollen, soil, and the Sudarium links suggests an ancient Middle Eastern origin that merits further exploration. My investigation, though not exhaustive, highlights some common-sense observations that build a case step by step, as we will get deeper into and throughout this book. The 1988 carbon-dating study, while significant in its methodology, is not conclusive due to identified flaws, prompting further scrutiny of the cloth's dating and context to reconcile conflicting data. The Shroud remains a profound enigma, inviting both skepticism and wonder, a puzzle that rewards persistent inquiry.

A personal journey into the mystery of the Shroud

Telegraph group Limited. London 1988

Chapter 3: The Carbon Dating of the Cloth

The most contentious issue surrounding the authenticity of the Shroud of Turin centers on the carbon dating tests conducted in 1988. Those results, placing the cloth between 1260 and 1390 AD, have shaped much of the modern debate. I recall reading a U.S. newspaper at the time declaring the Shroud a fraud, its sensational tone echoing global headlines. Initially, I dismissed the Shrouds' authenticity, skeptical of sweeping claims in light of the Catholic Church's long history with questionable relics. As one popular joke had it, the alleged fragments of the "true cross," if assembled, could rebuild Noah's Ark. Yet it was only through a deeper investigation that I uncovered the complexity of the carbon dating process and its results. Importantly, the Catholic Church never owned the Shroud, it remained with the Savoy family until 1983. Clearly, a context that tempers the Church's role in this controversy.

Three independent laboratories, Tucson, Zurich, and Oxford carried out the radiocarbon testing over several months in 1988. The coordinated effort was designed to ensure objectivity. Still, when the results indicated a medieval origin, the reaction was intense, sparking alternative explanations and critiques. Some researchers argued that bacterial or fungal biofilms may have introduced modern carbon, making the cloth appear centuries younger. While experiments show such contamination can affect Carbon 14 levels, most experts counter that the extent required enough to shift the Shroud's age by over a millennium would have been obvious under microscopy, yet no such evidence was reported. Others suggested the 1532 fire in Chambéry, with its intense heat and carbonized residue, may have altered the cloth's isotopic profile. While residue from the fire is acknowledged, peer-reviewed studies conclude that pre-treatment cleaning removed superficial contamination thus leaving little measurable effect. A third critique pointed to centuries of handling and restoration, which might have introduced newer carbon through oils or dust. But to shift the date by 1,200 years, contamination would need to constitute the majority of the tested sample, something that would have been both visible and documented.

Perhaps the strongest critique is that the tests relied on a single corner sample, an area heavily handled and possibly rewoven in medieval repairs. If true, the dated material may not reflect the Shroud's original cloth. Later reevaluations of the raw data, released in 2017, revealed serious issues: the results were statistically heterogeneous, some threads may have come from later repairs, and inconsistencies across the laboratories were improperly merged to produce an artificially narrow age range. The blind-test protocols were also abandoned, since the Shroud's distinctive weave made it easy to identify, leaving open the possibility of bias. These flaws suggest that the 1988 results may not be as conclusive as once reported.

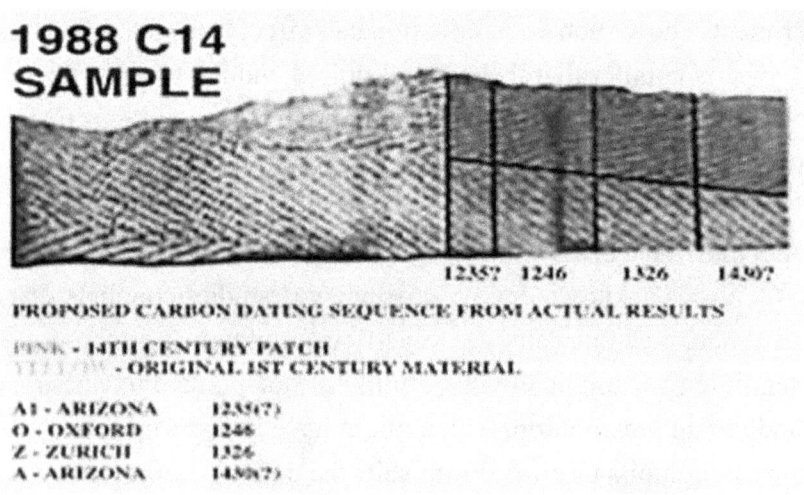

PROPOSED CARBON DATING SEQUENCE FROM ACTUAL RESULTS

PINK - 14TH CENTURY PATCH
      - ORIGINAL 1ST CENTURY MATERIAL

A1 - ARIZONA   1235(?)
O - OXFORD   1246
Z - ZURICH   1326
A - ARIZONA   1430(?)

Critics have long questioned the reliability of the 1988 radiocarbon dating of the Shroud of Turin, pointing out that the tests relied on a single sample, one that may have been repaired or contaminated from the corner area which is a site of known damage. This limitation, they argue, undermines the credibility of the entire analysis, as it may not represent the whole cloth's age. At the same time, the Church's reluctance to allow further sampling is understandable, since radiocarbon testing is inherently destructive and risks damaging a sacred relic, balancing preservation with scientific inquiry.

As with many major historical investigations, the Shroud controversy has unfolded not in a vacuum, of pure science, but in a tangle of politics, personalities, and money that influenced proceedings. Joseph G. Marino's book, 1988 C-14 Dating of the Shroud of Turin: A Stunning Exposé, documents behind-the-scenes disputes, questionable decisions, and even the influence of financial incentives that may have pressured outcomes. One detail has drawn particular scrutiny: a £1 million donation to Oxford University, reported by the Daily Telegraph on March 25, 1989. According to Marino, 45 businessmen and wealthy patrons pledged this sum to endow a professorship in Archaeological Sciences after Oxford's lab concluded that the Shroud was a medieval artifact, raising questions about motivation.

The timing of the donation has sparked debate, especially since it coincided with Dr. Michael Tite, formerly the British Museum's independent overseer of the Shroud dating, assuming leadership of the Oxford laboratory. A transition that seemed too convenient. Critics have speculated whether the donation was a reward for the "medieval" verdict, implying undue influence. However, Marino clarifies that the original reporting, the gift framed as a means of securing Oxford's research future after Professor Edward Hall's retirement, not as a direct incentive tied to the Shroud results. Though the proximity fuels suspicion. Whether the circumstances were suspicious or simply coincidental remains open to interpretation, highlighting the human elements in scientific endeavors.

> A reexamination of the data uncovered several
> critical statistical flaws that erode confidence:

A strong heterogeneity among sample groups (p-value < 0.0001) demonstrated that they were not statistically homogeneous, raising doubts about the validity of assigning a single date range to the entire Shroud, as variations suggest inconsistencies. Early statistical methods misapplied chi-squared analysis, neglecting systematic errors and thus masking potential biases in the aggregation process. The original sample was small (about 7 cm by 1 cm) and possibly included repair material from 16th-century restorations, violating the assumption that it represented the entire cloth's uniformity. Inconsistent data were improperly merged, skewing mean date calculations and leading to an artificially narrow confidence interval. Initial handling of data lacked thorough scrutiny; inconsistencies only became evident after the 2017 Freedom of Information Act release, which disclosed raw data previously withheld.

The peer-reviewed rebuttals collectively reinforce that scientifically accepted dating methods remain robust, reliable, and well-supported against creationist dissent. Which often stems from misunderstandings, misapplications, and ideological biases rather than scientific evidence. Although radiocarbon dating is a powerful tool for chronology, its results are open to debate based on sampling, contamination, calibration, and regional environmental factors that can introduce variability. These issues fuel ongoing discussions, particularly around complex or high-profile artifacts like the Shroud of Turin, where stakes are high. Together, these statistical and procedural flaws cast serious doubt on the 1988 radiocarbon dating results, suggesting the medieval conclusion may not hold under renewed scrutiny. Issues such as sample heterogeneity, systematic error, poor sampling, and inadequate data analysis undermine confidence in those conclusions, calling for advanced retesting.

Technology Evolves

From 2019 to 2024, new research using Wide-Angle X-ray Scattering (WAXS) was conducted by scientists in Bari, Italy, offering a fresh perspective on the Shroud's age. This innovative, non-destructive technique examines the microscopic structure and degradation of linen fibers, providing insights into natural aging processes. Applying WAXS to a tiny fiber from the Shroud, the results suggest an approximate fabric age of 2,000 years, consistent with the era of Jesus Christ. Findings that conflict with the 1988 medieval dating, as the degradation patterns match first-century samples.

The WAXS technique employs X-rays, akin to radiographic scans used in medicine, to probe the fabric and evaluate cellulose fiber degradation at the molecular level. The observed degradation matches that of ancient linen, similar to cloth samples retrieved from historic sites like Masada in Israel, where artifacts from the Roman period provide benchmarks. This alignment strengthens the case for an ancient origin, contrasting with carbon dating's finding.

However, WAXS has limitations that warrant caution: It relies on extrapolating degradation rates, which may be affected by environmental or conservation conditions over centuries, such as exposure to light or humidity in storage. The findings are based on a very small fiber sample, raising concerns about representativeness without wider testing to confirm consistency across the cloth. Independent verification is necessary to confirm and validate these results, as replication by other labs would bolster credibility. The method infers age indirectly by material deterioration rather than direct calendar dating, with potential variability due to differing aging environments like temperature fluctuations. The findings continue to fuel debate among both scientific and faith-based communities, as evidence remains inconclusive regarding the Shroud's full authenticity, highlighting the need for complementary methods.

WAXS X-ray testing provides compelling evidence suggesting the Shroud's age could be around 2,000 years, challenging the earlier medieval dating by offering a non-isotopic alternative. Nevertheless, the dependence on fiber degradation modeling and the limited sample size emphasizes the need for further study. To resolve ongoing questions about the Shroud of Turin's true age and authenticity the results need to be integrated with supporting data. After reviewing the Shroud's historical provenance, chain of custody, and the most pertinent dating techniques from carbon to X-ray, no conclusive evidence emerges to definitively link this artifact as the burial cloth of Jesus of Nazareth, though patterns intrigue. While historians may fill gaps with reasonable hypotheses based upon biblical records, including intriguing correlations such as the Sudarium, the Shroud sharing the same blood type AB and digitally matched blood patterns that overlay precisely. This remains insufficient proof of its status as Christ's burial cloth, requiring more to convince skeptics.

Chapter 4: The Image

Turning to the image itself, the Shroud measures approximately 14 feet three inches long by 3 feet seven inches wide, an unusual size unless considered using ancient measurements such as the cubit, a standard in biblical times. Using the Assyrian cubit of about 21 inches, the Shroud measures about 8 cubits long by 2 cubits wide, hinting at a connection to the ancient Near East and possibly the first century, where such dimensions would fit customary burial practices. The faint, yellowish-brown image depicts a naked man with both front and back views and is barely visible to the naked eye, requiring optimal lighting for clarity. These views are believed to represent a man laid on the cloth, with the fabric then drawn over his head and down the front in a traditional wrapping, creating a double imprint. Despite its faintness, the image reveals wounds and bloodstains identified as type AB, a blood type prevalent in the Middle East and rare in medieval Europe, adding to its enigmatic profile. Viewing the Shroud up close, the image details are less discernible than when seen from 6 to 8 feet away, where the overall form emerges, a property that puzzled early observers. Notably, the image possesses characteristics of a photographic negative, where light and dark areas reverse to reveal a positive likeness. This discovery traces back to May 28, 1898, when Italian lawyer and amateur photographer Secondo Pia took the first photographs of the Shroud of Turin during an exhibition authorized by King Humbert I of Italy, using glass plates exposed under electric lights. Upon developing the photographic plates in his darkroom, Pia found that the negative image revealed a clearer, positive depiction of the man, with details like facial features and wounds clearly visible to the naked eye, transforming a faint stain into a lifelike portrait. This photographic revelation sparked modern scientific interest in the Shroud, shifting it from devotional object to subject of empirical study. Pia's work, using early photographic techniques and electric lighting for the first time on the relic, was initially met with a mix of awe and skepticism, as it suggested properties beyond known art. His photographic negative remains a foundational contribution to sindonology, the study of the Shroud, pioneering image analysis. The significant detail enhancement from the negative images inspired investigations across scientific and historical disciplines, launching a century of research.

The detail of the scourge wounds clearly indicates the wounds were inflicted by a Roman flagrum, a weapon designed for maximum suffering.

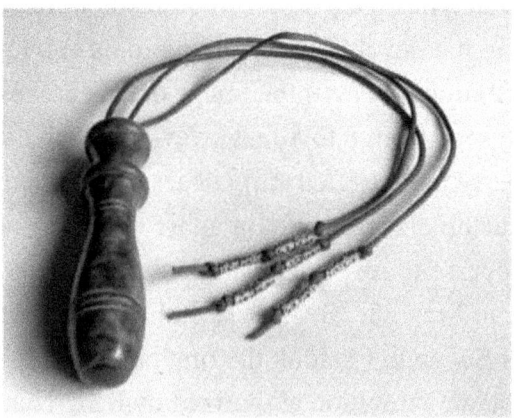

The Flagrum is a type of lash that has three leather straps with small lead dumbbell-shaped tips that dig into the skin when struck, tearing flesh with each blow. The dumbbell-shaped wounds are clearly visible on the image, matching historical descriptions of Roman execution tools. Forensic analysis also determined that the man in the image was struck by two men, one being taller than the other, as evidenced by varying heights of the marks. Further details reveal that unlike most crucifixion victims, whose legs were broken to hasten death, his legs were not broken, aligning with Gospel accounts. The Romans used this technique to speed up death since the victim needed to push up with their legs to continue breathing, a grueling process; this man's intact legs suggest a prolonged ordeal. This man also had a cap of thorns, not a wreath.

Unlike the pictures depicting Jesus's wreath-type crown, this cap was a complete head covering, inferred from the distribution of injuries. This conclusion comes from the bloodstains and puncture marks visible across the entire scalp, from the forehead to the back and nape of the neck, not just around the temples where a wreath would rest, indicating full encirclement. Over 50 distinct puncture wounds are observable on the Shroud's head area, each a testament to brutality. The pattern of blood stains, including large ones at the forehead and groups at the nape, indicate thorns penetrated deeply, injuring arteries and veins across the scalp, causing profuse bleeding. There also appears to be a stab wound from a Roman spear with a three-inch-wide head, post-mortem as described in John 19:34. There are several divergences from accepted traditional depictions of the crucifixion of Jesus. The nails through the wrists versus the hands, palm nail placement would fail underweight, and the crown of thorns being a full cap versus the laurel donut- shaped crown in art, challenging artistic conventions with forensic realism.

This reminded me of my deep dive into the Billy the Kid story, where I noticed something similar in challenging established narratives. The claimant account I studied described the layout of the Lincoln County courthouse in a way that didn't match what we see there today or the accounts of authors and historians, initially seeming erroneous. At first, that raised questions, but as I looked closer the claimant's version actually made more sense logically, forensically and historically. Challenging what most people took for granted and far more believable than the so-called "common knowledge," much like the Shroud's details upend traditional views. Additionally, the financial benefit accruing to the Fort Sumner town also, may have influenced the search for the truth, similar to what we see with the Shroud, where tourism and devotion play roles. The Shroud challenged what most people took for granted and felt far more believable than the so-called "common knowledge," as the Shroud's details upend traditional views.

The reason why a crucified man would not have nails driven into the palms of the hands is because the body weight would tear through the flesh, causing failure; the wrists are supported by bone and can hold the weight, a fact known to Roman executioners. The Roman soldiers would also not take time fashioning a crown; they more likely would take a bunch of thorn plants and crush the center into a cap and smash it onto the victim's head for mockery. These are relatively small observations but looking deeper, more details come forward that build a cohesive picture. The level of detail of the Shroud is surprising and similar to a photograph in resolution. The bruises both on the shoulder and face coincide with the description in the biblical texts of carrying the cross and beating. The image complete with scourge marks over the entire body and the corresponding blood stains is actually beyond what is in the biblical accounts, adding layers not explicitly stated. I wondered if even Michelangelo with his knowledge of the human body would know that the nails through the wrists would cause the thumbs to fold in as depicted on the Shroud due to median nerve damage, a subtle anatomical accuracy. The blood trails and pooling are consistent with a man crucified vertically and then laid horizontally, with flows defying gravity in life but settling in death. Analysis by a forensic doctor verified these facts as consistent with real trauma. The proportions of the image are incredibly accurate, with body metrics matching a 1st-century male. Critics say that the fingers appear too long but upon examination the fingers appear to be depicted, almost, with an X-ray effect making them appear longer, revealing underlying structures. This is also observed around the mouth where the teeth appear as if X-rayed from the inside out, suggesting internal radiation emission. In fact, during a presentation of the image, a dentist in the audience observed the similarities to X-rays taken within film inside the mouth, where radiation penetrates from the outside to the inside This suggests radiation coming from within the body with the linen acting as the film as opposed to a dental office where radiation is supplied outside of the body with the film inside the mouth, inverting the process. That is an interesting concept but dead bodies do not emit radiation; or do they under extraordinary circumstances?

The Study of the Image Goes High-Tech

This marks the start of a scientific journey from which I never recovered, a path that blended my analytical past with profound personal questions. If my experience is any indication, prepare Yourself, you're in for a remarkable ride that challenges Preconceptions. The story begins with the VP8 Image Analyzer, invented in 1972 by Peter Schumacher of Interpretation Systems Incorporated for advanced visualization. This analog device processes images by converting brightness (luminance) levels into vertical relief, effectively creating "height maps" that render images in 3D. Originally developed for use in technical and scientific applications such as X-ray analysis for medical diagnostics, radar interpretation for military navigation, infrared thermography for heat detection, laser profiling for surface mapping, and earth resource satellite imaging for environmental monitoring. The VP8 offered a novel way to visualize data beyond two dimensions.

Unlike digital converters that rely on software algorithms, the VP8 image analyzer translates photographic image density, variations in light and dark areas into vertical relief, creating a topographic map with realistic shadows and highlights that mimic physical depth. For typical photographs, this process produces distorted, inaccurate renderings, as photographic luminance merely reflects surface lighting conditions and angles rather than true topography. However, in 1976, scientists at Sandia Laboratories achieved an extraordinary result when they processed a 1931 photograph of the face on the Shroud of Turin using the VP8 on the high-quality black-and-white image. While standard photographs yield chaotic patterns of light and dark when analyzed by the VP8, resulting in warped figures, the Shroud's image produced an anatomically accurate, three-dimensional topographic relief of a human figure, result unprecedented for any conventional photograph, suggesting encoded spatial information.

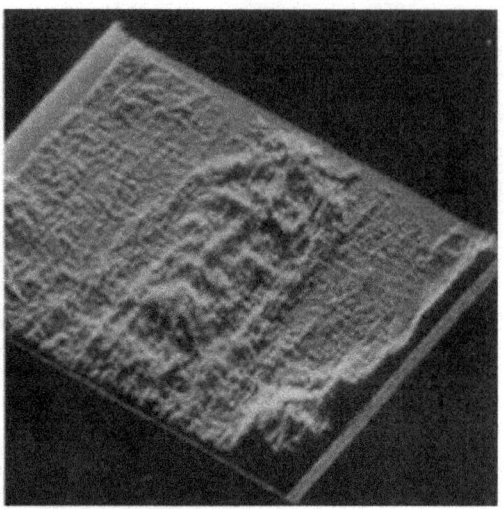

3D image of Turin Shroud from VP-8 image analyzer

Initially, I hypothesized that a medium like a charcoal drawing, with its gradual shading from light to dark, might replicate the gradient effect that enabled the VP8's response, assuming artistic technique. This assumption was incorrect upon deeper review. The Shroud's image exhibits a distinctive "halftone effect," a phenomenon akin to halftone printing in newspapers, where images are formed not by smooth tonal gradations but by patterns of dots varying in density to create the illusion of shades when viewed from a distance, a method used since the 19th century for image reproduction. On the Shroud, this effect arises from yellowish discoloration affecting only the outermost fibers of the linen threads, a superficial change. The discoloration is not continuous across fibers or threads but occurs in discrete, localized spots on the surface, varying in distribution like pixels. The perceived intensity (lightness or darkness) of any area depends primarily on the number of discolored fibers per unit area, not on variations in the depth or intensity of the discoloration itself, creating uniform color in affected spots. Thus, "darker" regions simply contain more discolored fibers, not more intensely colored ones, a binary-like system.

This halftone effect creates the appearance of smooth gradients at a macro scale, despite being composed of a mosaic of uniformly colored fibers distributed sparsely or densely, much like digital images at low resolution. Viewed from a distance, the image gains clarity, much like halftone newspaper images that appear sharper from afar, resolving into coherent forms. Microscopically, all discolored fibers share a similar hue, with no variation in shade at this scale, confirming consistency. The three-dimensional visual effect and variations in shading at larger scales result entirely from the spatial arrangement of these fibers, not chemical gradients. This characteristic sets the Shroud's image apart from those created by conventional painting, dyeing, or burning, where color depth or intensity typically varies continuously or results from different chemical processes like oxidation or charring, leaving residues.

The Shroud of Turin's halftone effect refers to its unique image formation, where perceived shades and intensity arise from the density of uniformly discolored fibers rather than continuous tonal variations or differing color depths, a property that defies replication. The image demonstrates accurately how light behaves and how distance affects brightness. The image also contains mathematically precise ratios that are consistent under different types of light. This phenomenon is fundamental to both the image's formation and its striking visual impact, contributing to its photographic negative quality.

The VP8 results captivated researchers Dr. Eric Jumper and Dr. John Jackson, aerospace engineers with a knack for image analysis. Dr. Jackson was inspired by these findings but initially skeptical; he was attributed as saying "Give me 15 minutes and the scientific method and I will prove the Shroud is a hoax," reflecting his rigorous approach. Dr. Jackson formed the Shroud of Turin Research Project (STURP) in the months that followed, assembling a team of experts. Two years later, in 1978, the team conducted the first comprehensive scientific examination of the Shroud during a rare access period. For in-depth details on the VP8 and STURP, I highly recommend shroud.com, founded by Barrie Schwortz (1946–2024), a member of the STURP team and a respected photographer whose documentation was invaluable.

Barrie's story deserves special mention as it exemplifies open-minded inquiry. Invited by Dr. Alan Adler, a biophysicist at Los Alamos National Laboratory, Barrie was initially reluctant to join the project, noting, "Alan, I'm Jewish, this isn't really my area," wary of religious implications. To which Alan replied, "I am Jewish, too, but there's important, non-religious science to do," emphasizing empirical focus. With the promise of a purely scientific study and the participation of over 30 scientists from various backgrounds, including atheists and believers, Barrie agreed, changing the course of his career and deepening his appreciation for the Shroud, even as he remained true to his heritage, documenting without bias.

Notably, STURP drew specialists from institutions known for cutting-edge research, such as Los Alamos National Laboratory for nuclear expertise and Jet Propulsion Laboratories for imaging technology sites associated with the development of destructive technologies like atomic bombs. All brought together ironically to examine what may be one of history's most important artifacts, symbolizing peace. To be clear, the STURP team was given permission to analyze the Shroud by the Savoy royal family, who owned it at the time not the Catholic Church or the Pope, avoiding ecclesiastical interference. The ownership was not transferred to the Pope until the death of King Umberto II in 1983, when it became Vatican property.

Chapter 5: The STURP Team Scientific Disciplines

The STURP team included a diverse array of experts to cover all angles:

Physics: Analysis of cloth and image properties, including light interaction.

Chemistry: Fabric composition and possible reactions responsible for image formation, testing for pigments.

Forensic Pathology: Study of wounds, bloodstains, and body image for realism.

Photography: Detailed documentation and image analysis using advanced techniques.

Thermal Chemistry & Imaging: Investigation of heat effects and image development through simulations.

Optical Physics: Assessment of light transmission and image characteristics like negativity.

Electrical Engineering: Technical support and instrumentation for measurements.

Infrared Spectroscopy: Chemical analysis of image and cloth for molecular changes.

Hematology, Microscopy, Nuclear Physics, Forensic Medical Science, Radiation Science: Specialized analyses covering blood composition, microscopic detail, atomic interactions, medical evidence, and radiation effects on materials.

Notable STURP Team Members included:

John P. Jackson (STURP President, physicist, U.S. Air Force Academy), lead on image theory.

Eric J. Jumper (STURP Vice President, aeronautics, U.S. Air Force Academy), co-developer of VP8 applications.

William Mottern (Sandia National Laboratory), expert in image processing.

Raymond N. Rogers (Los Alamos National Laboratory), chemist on fiber analysis.

Don Lynn (Jet Propulsion Laboratory), specialist in spectral imaging.

Barrie Schwortz (photographer), capturing high-fidelity records.

Sam Pellicori (optical physicist), studying light properties.

Robert Bucklin (forensic pathologist), verifying wounds.

Additional specialists included conservationists and chemists from varied institutions, ensuring comprehensive coverage.

The team spent five days—120 hours total—examining the Shroud, working in three daily shifts to maximize data collection under time constraints, using portable labs.

A leading scientific hypothesis proposes that the image on the Shroud of Turin was formed by a burst of directional radiation emitted from within the body wrapped in the cloth, a theory that explains its precision. This theory centers on the idea that either ultraviolet light, particle radiation, or a similarly energetic mechanism projected outward in a vertical, collimated direction, both upwards and downwards, producing the highly resolved image seen on both the front and back without distortion.

Directional Radiation Hypothesis

John Jackson's research and later nuclear physicists argue that radiation was not random, but rather vertically collimated, meaning each point on the cloth received energy from only one point on the body directly underneath it, like a point-source projection. This prevents lateral diffusion and explains why the image is so exact, with encoded three-dimensional spatial information, including faint features like bones beneath the skin visible in enhanced views. The hypothesis contends that this energy altered the chemical bonds in the cellulose at the outer layer of the linen fibers, causing the observed discrete discoloration through oxidation, a superficial change.

Types of Radiation and Experimental Support

Experiments have shown that UV lasers, excimer lasers at 193 nm wavelength, and particle radiation (protons and neutrons) can create surface-level effects similar to the finely-resolved image present on the Shroud, discoloring fibers without penetration. But the energy requirements far exceed anything available in history or nature, involving trillions of watts concentrated into an instantaneous flash, akin to a nuclear event but localized. The image also includes areas not in contact with the body, up to 3.7 cm away, indicating a non-contact, remote process consistent with energetic radiation radiating outwards from the form.

Implications and Scientific Summary

- The directional radiation theory addresses how the Shroud encodes front and dorsal images with high vertical resolution (0.2 micrometers) and three-dimensional detail without damaging the cloth or leaving residues.

- The image is present only on the microscopic uppermost fibers (200-600 nm depth), suggesting the effect was highly superficial and controlled, unlike heat or chemicals.

- These findings, while not universally accepted due to the supernatural implications, represent the best attempt to scientifically explain the image's origin without recourse to pigment, vapor, heat, or manual contact, fitting observed data.

In sum, the directional radiation hypothesis suggests intense, vertically projected energy from the body as the mechanism behind the Shroud of Turin's enigmatic image, a model that integrates multiple lines of evidence.

Key Findings of the STURP Study

The image depicts a real human figure, a scourged and crucified Man, not the work of an artist, as no directionality of brush strokes or pigments was found. The image is superficial, existing on the outermost fibers (top 200 nm) and does not penetrate the cloth, preserving the weave's integrity. There is no evidence of paint, dye, pigment, or scorch marks on the image areas, ruled out by chemical tests. Bloodstains contain genuine human blood components, including hemoglobin, bilirubin (indicating trauma), and serum albumin (Blood type AB), with pre- and post-mortem flows.

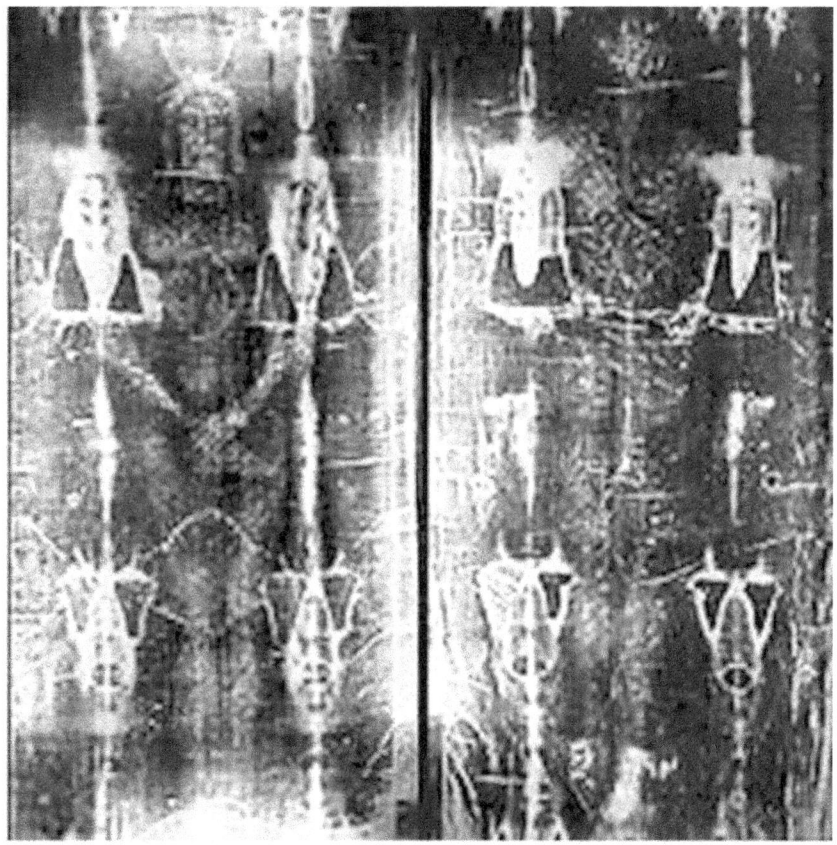

The Shroud of Turin ©1978 Barrie M. Schwortz

The image depicts a real human figure, a scourged and crucified man, not the work of an artist.

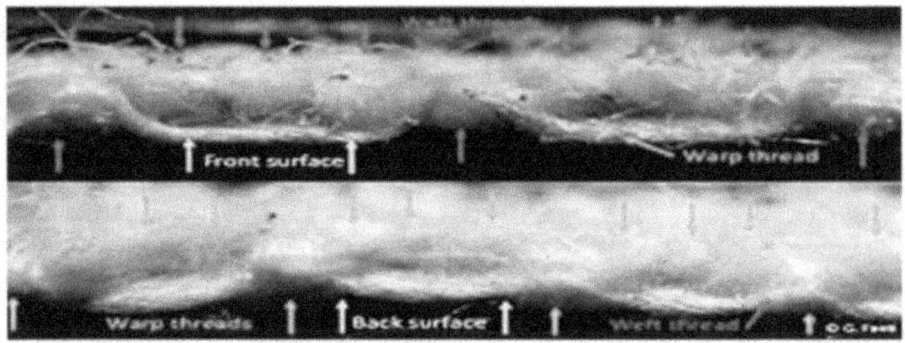

Two cross sections of Vercelli's TS facsimile in which warp and weft treads are evidenced © Fanti

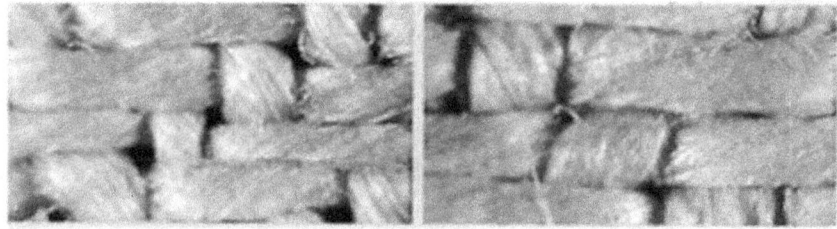

There is no evidence of paint, dye, pigment, or scorch marks on the image.

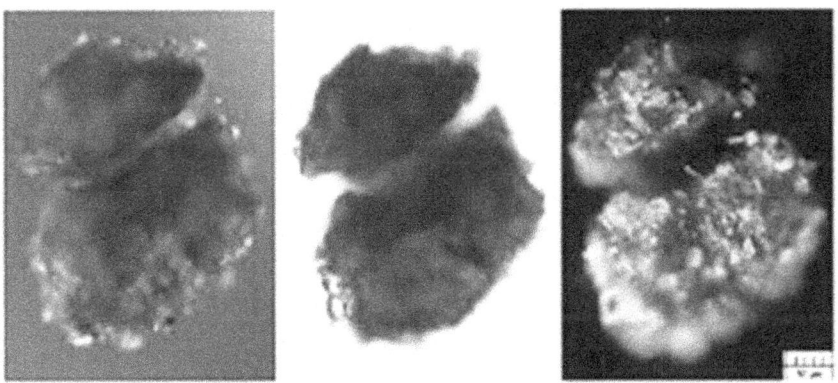

Bloodstains contain genuine human blood components, including hemoglobin and serum albumin (Blood type AB).

Dr. Kelly Kearse, scientist and researcher, critically examined the forensic biochemical and serological aspects of the Shroud's bloodstains, addressing challenges in ancient sample analysis. He helped highlight important scientific questions about the Shroud's authenticity and image formation through peer-reviewed work. Dr. Kelly Kearse has published several scientific papers and articles on the Shroud of Turin, focusing mainly on the analysis of bloodstains, their nature, and challenges in forensic and serological testing for aged materials. Some of her key publications include:

☐ "Unanticipated issues in serological analysis of blood species: The Shroud of Turin as a case example" (2020). This paper discusses difficulties in analyzing blood species from aged samples using traditional serological methods, noting degradation effects.

- "A Simple, Natural Mechanism for the Transfer of Dry Bloodstains onto the Shroud of Turin" (2023). Published in the International Journal of Archaeology, this paper explains a natural mechanism for how bloodstains could transfer to the cloth via contact and clotting.

- "Inadequacies in Serological ABO Typing of Ancient Artifacts: The Shroud of Turin as a Case Example" (2023). This commentary highlights limitations in blood typing on ancient artifacts like the Shroud, due to contamination and age.

- "Blood clotting, serum halo rings, and the bloodstains on the Shroud of Turin". A detailed study analyzing clotting patterns and serum halo rings around bloodstains, consistent with real wounds.

- "Blood Transfer to the Shroud of Turin: The Washing Hypothesis Revisited" (2025). Published in the International Journal of Archaeology, this paper reexamines whether the body was washed before being placed in the Shroud, based on blood transfer evidence and flow patterns.

The process that created the image remains unexplained by current chemical or physical methods; it is still a scientific mystery to the present day, resisting replication. The data collected by STURP established the foundation for all subsequent research on the Shroud, influencing decades of studies.

The STURP final report concluded:

"We can conclude for now that the Shroud image is that of a real human form of a scourged, crucified man. It is not the product of an artist. The blood stains are composed of hemoglobin and also give a positive test for serum albumin. The image is an ongoing mystery and until further chemical studies are made...the problem remains unsolved."

Basically, we don't know how this image was created nor can we duplicate it with known techniques. Does this mean the Shroud takes its place among the Pyramids or Stonehenge as an ancient wonder? Could we in the 21st century using modern equipment and technology build Stonehenge or a Pyramid from scratch? I am not sure, but the originals stand as a humbling testament to the limits of modern science. In the case of the Shroud, actual attempts are being made in the 20th and 21st century failing to replicate the Shroud's image despite advanced tools. The result of this analysis is that we can't duplicate the Shroud using 20th-century technology and the same is true to date in the 21st century, even with lasers and AI. The Shroud's image appears to have been formed by an energy event that modern physics cannot explain.

Despite ruling out painting, photography, or scorched techniques through exhaustive tests, the question remains: What is the Shroud and how was its image formed? What is remarkable is that over 30 top scientists who studied the Shroud around the clock with the most sophisticated equipment known at the time walked away saying whatever it is, it was not made by human hands. This is a consensus from diverse experts. To date, no one has managed to duplicate the image using 21st-century technology, despite efforts with high-energy sources. The image is extremely superficial, it affects only the top 2% of the linen fibers (about 0.2 micrometers), while the bloodstains penetrate the cloth up to 20 threads, indicating sequence. Significantly, the blood was deposited before the image, further undermining any artistic explanation, as this would require applying real blood, both pre- and post-mortem, in anatomically precise locations and then overlaying a negative image that matches the wounds described in the Gospels with microscopic detail. The artist would also have required a microscope since the level of detail is not visible until the image is photographically reversed, an anachronism for medieval times. Researchers have considered natural processes involving body fluids, decomposition products, and gases as possible explanations, but each has flaws. Some of the prominent theories are summarized below, evaluated for strengths and weaknesses:

Vapors or Gases from Body Fluids

Paul Vignon (1902, 1937): Suggested that ammonia vapors from the breakdown of urea in sweat interacted with burial spices (aloes and myrrh) on the cloth, forming an image without direct contact through chemical reaction. Laboratory experiments produced faint imprints after 10 minutes to 24 hours at room temperature, though such processes would require specific conditions: (body temperature around 37°C, humidity, timing before decomposition).

Raymond N. Rogers & Arnoldi (2002–2003): Proposed a Maillard reaction, where amino compounds from the corpse's sweat or decomposition reacted with sugar residues from ancient linen manufacturing (vanillin loss), forming a superficial coloration similar to the Shroud's yellowing.

However, later analysis found no proteins or bodily fluids in the image areas, challenging the hypothesis and leaving gaps in chemical traces.

Decomposition Products and Chemical Reactions

Giulio Fazio & Giuseppe Mandaglio (2021): Supported the Maillard reaction but emphasized the role of thermal energy from the body and cellulose degradation by corpse emissions, modeling diffusion. Giulio Fanti et al. (2010–2011): Compiled evidence for vapor or decomposition-based formation mechanisms, suggesting gases from fermentation, though results remain inconclusive without full replication.

Eric J. Jumper, Alan D. Adler, et al. (1984): Analyzed stain formation, suggesting blood appeared before the faint body image, indicating a two-stage process where fluids set first, then image formed.

Direct Contact or Fluid Transfer

John A. DeSalvo (1982), Jean Volckringer (1991): Drew analogies to plant impressions in herbariums and proposed direct transfer of body fluids during wrapping, imprinting through sweat and oils.

G. De Liso (2000–2002): Conducted experiments showing image formation on linen treated with burial spices under simulated earthquake conditions, hypothesizing seismic energy acceleration. On the day of the crucifixion an earthquake took place in Jerusalem which created the seismic energy.

Timing and Condition

Research consistently suggests that, for vapors or decomposition products to create the image, the body must have remained wrapped for 24–48 hours under warm, humid conditions to allow reactions—but no more than 72 hours to prevent fluid stains from putrefaction, aligning with biblical timelines. Body temperature (postmortem cooling) and environmental conditions critically affect reaction rates, with models showing optimal windows.

Despite extensive study, no consensus has emerged, and every naturalistic hypothesis faces significant challenges, such as the Shroud's unique 3D imaging properties (distance-correlated intensity) and the lack of residues where the image appears, like no directional fibers.

The STURP team in their analysis:

Reported Flaws in the Vapor Graphic Theory (e.g., Vignon's Hypothesis)

This hypothesis suggests ammonia vapors from urea in sweat or early decomposition interact with burial spices like aloes on the linen to form the image through diffusion, essentially a chemical imprint.

Distortion from Cloth Draping: The cloth would naturally drape over the body, leading to contact in some areas and gaps in others (up to 3 cm), causing image distortions from uneven exposure. However, the Shroud's image shows no such wrapping distortions, appearing as a vertical projection inconsistent with vapor diffusion over uneven surfaces, which would blur contours.

• Blurring from Lateral Diffusion: Vapors like ammonia would diffuse laterally (sideways) as well as vertically, resulting in a blurred, low-resolution image rather than the sharp, high-resolution details observed on the Shroud (e.g., facial features at 0.5 mm resolution).

• Lack of Chemical Evidence: No traces of ammonia, urea derivatives, or aloes have been detected on the Shroud via microchemical tests (e.g., STURP 1978-1981 findings using spectroscopy), undermining the required reactants for the reaction.

• Incompatibility with Image Superficiality and Fluorescence: Vapors should penetrate beyond the topmost fibers (diffusion depth >1 mm), but the image is confined to a 200-600 nm depth without fluorescence in image areas, which vapor-induced reactions might produce through byproducts.

• Failure to Explain 3D Properties: The image encodes 3D information (via VP-8 analyzer), correlating intensity with cloth-body distance (inverse square law), but vapor diffusion lacks a mechanism for this precise encoding and would homogenize intensity across gaps. [42]

• No Side or Backside Imaging: Vapors from the whole body should produce side images or color the cloth's backside through permeation, but the Shroud shows only frontal/dorsal views with no backside imaging or lateral marks.

Experimental replications (e.g., using ammonia exposure in chambers) have produced blurred results with convection perturbations, failing to match the Shroud's resolution or 3D encoding. Some researchers, as of 2025, continue to debate the possibility of alternative explanations, including radiation-based mechanisms that better fit data.

Flaws in General Decomposition and Body Fluids Hypotheses (e.g., Fanti, Fazio, DeSalvo, Volckringer)

These suggest gases, vapors, or fluids from decomposition or direct contact form the image, often via chemical reactions like oxidation.

- No Evidence of Decomposition Products: STURP found no biochemicals from decay (e.g., no putrefaction gases or amines around lips/orifices), contradicting hypotheses requiring corpse emissions; blood is present but separate from the image, with no overlap.

- Penetration and Superficiality Mismatch: Fluids/gases would penetrate deeper than the observed 200-600 nm surface layer via capillary action; no cementation or flow traces detected in image areas.

- Inconsistent Blood and Image Properties: Bloodstains are real (with proteins, bilirubin from trauma), but image areas lack fluids/proteins or DNA; blood formed first (clotted), but no smearing if body unwashed, and reddish color unexplained naturally (blood typically browns over time).

- Lack of Side Images and Distortions: Direct contact or gases should produce side/body images and gravity-based density differences (frontal vs. dorsal weight), but none observed, with uniform resolution.

• Experimental Replication Failures: Attempts (e.g., herbarium analogies with plants, earthquake simulations with vibrations) don't replicate 3D encoding, high resolution, or absence of borders/distortions, yielding inferior results.

• Conflict with Radiocarbon Dating: Dated to medieval (1260-1390 AD) by C14, but hypotheses assume 1st-century context with body fluids; invisible mending theories disputed by microscopy, though contamination persists as issue.

Flaws in Time Frame Arguments (24-72 Hours)

• Timing Paradox with Decomposition: Estimates require enough time for vapors/gases to build but removal before liquids exude, yet no putrefaction evidence (bloating, stains) suggests insufficient decomposition occurred within the window.

• Variable Conditions Not Accounted For: Assumes specific temperatures (e.g., 41°C postmortem for reactions), but cooler tombs (Jerusalem Spring 15°C) would extend times beyond biblical/ historical windows (39 hours from death to discovery), risking unobserved decay or no image.

• Lack of Empirical Basis: Derived from forensics/experiments on modern cadavers, not Shroud testing; inconsistencies like no backside imaging challenge gas accumulation over time, as diffusion would affect all sides.

Radiation Theory

There are no scientifically confirmed instances of the human body naturally emitting significant radiation after death; however, two niche forms of emission are known: biophoton emission ceases at death, and radioactivity can persist when a person has been exposed to or treated with radioactive substances before death, both rare cases.

Living organisms emit ultra-weak photon emission (UPE), a faint glow from biological processes like oxidation, that vanishes after death as metabolism halts. Studies using sensitive cameras found visible light emissions from live mice, which dropped dramatically and essentially disappeared after euthanasia, even when their body temperature was artificially maintained to simulate life. This phenomenon, called biophoton emission, appears linked to metabolic reactions and reactive oxygen species in cells. After death, these reactions stop, causing the light emission to cease abruptly, measured in lux as near zero. These emissions are extremely faint, far below what is visible to the human eye (10^{-15} W/cm^2) specifically meaning, the amount of power (in watts) delivered per square centimeter of area, or one quadrillionth of a watt per square centimeter and are not considered hazardous or a form of radiation in the traditional, dangerous, sense like ionizing rays.

Radioactive contamination can occur in very specific cases, such as medical treatments. If a person recently received nuclear medicine therapies or implants for cancer, their body may retain radioactive material post-mortem, decaying slowly. Cremains (ashes) from such bodies have, in rare cases, shown detectable radioactivity, but usually at low, regulated levels below safety thresholds. If death occurs soon after cancer radiotherapy involving radioactive implants or certain injected radiopharmaceuticals like iodine-131, the deceased may emit ionizing radiation for a period after death, requiring special handling. Accidents, nuclear incidents like Chernobyl, or exposure to radioactive materials can also result in a body that remains radioactive after death until the material decays or is removed, as seen in forensic cases.

Outside these exceptional scenarios, no other form of hazardous electromagnetic radiation is known to be emitted from human bodies after death, limiting natural explanations.

The body ceases its natural ultra-weak light emission upon death, and radioactive emission after death is seen only in rare cases of radioactive exposure or medical treatment before death, neither fitting the Shroud. What would it take to create a superficial image similar to the Shroud? The key considerations are that the image must be limited to the topmost fibers (superficial), stable over centuries without fading, and not result from burning, which would char or weaken the linen.

Creation a superficial, Shroud-like image with radiation. You would need controlled conditions: Use short, intense pulses of ultraviolet (preferably far-UV at 193 nm) radiation, typically from a suitable laser like an excimer, to target surface layers.

Tune the parameters (intensity ~10^9 W/cm^2, duration ~50 ns, energy density ~1 J/cm^2) with great precision to oxidize cellulose without penetration.

Terms in plain language

Intensity: (~10^9 W/cm^2): This is power per area at the peak of the pulse; it tells how quickly energy is delivered to each square centimeter while the pulse is on (higher means more "instantaneous punch").

Duration: (~50 ns): The pulse length; 50 nanoseconds is 50 billionths of a second, so the pulse is extremely brief.

Energy density: (~1 J/cm^2): Also called fluence; it's the total energy delivered to each square centimeter over the entire pulse (intensity integrated over time).

Ensure the fabric is linen (ideally untreated ancient flax), so the image remains on the outermost fibril surfaces, as modern synthetics react differently. These methods have shown the closest results to the image superficiality and other unusual characteristics seen on the Shroud of Turin, like negativity and 3D encoding, though full replication eludes.

Radiation-Based Methods for Superficial Image Creation: Expanded Explanation

Ultraviolet Laser or Light Exposure on Linen. Mechanism: When linen fibers are exposed to intense ultraviolet (UV) radiation pulses, especially from excimer lasers operating at specific wavelengths like 193 nm argon-fluoride, the energy is absorbed predominantly by the outermost molecular layers of the fibers due to shallow penetration depth. This absorption results in breaking chemical bonds mainly in cellulose, causing photochemical oxidation and dehydration that yellows the surface. Crucially, these changes occur only within the primary cell wall, which is extremely thin (less than 0.1 mm thick), ensuring the rest of the fiber remains unaffected and the weave intact, mimicking the Shroud's profile.

Superficiality: This restricted effect creates a superficial discoloration limited to 200-600 nm, matching STURP observations, without heat damage or deeper alteration, as UV excites electrons without thermal transfer.

Science has discovered that it would take 34 trillion watts of energy expended in 1/40 of a nanosecond to create the image.

Challenges of Distance and Timing:

• The Shroud draped over a body with varying cloth-to-body distances, including spots approximately 1.5 inches (1.575 inches) away from the surface.

• Light travels roughly 11.8 billion inches per second, meaning it takes about 0.1335 nanoseconds to cross 1.575 inches.

• A theory limiting the flash duration to 1/40th of a nanosecond (0.025 ns) to prevent heat damage implies the flash would have to somehow affect areas faster than light could travel the gap.

• According to established physics and relativity, nothing can travel faster than the speed of light, making this aspect of the hypothesis physically implausible within known natural laws.

• This contradiction remains a significant challenge and a key point in the ongoing mystery surrounding the Shroud's image formation.

Radiation-based image formation hypothesis on linen involves an extremely brief, intense burst of UV or VUV radiation that alters the superficial fibers chemically without heat damage, reproducing the Shroud's unique superficial and 3D imaging traits. Experimental laser studies support the feasibility of superficial discoloration but expose the enormous physical and energetic challenges to replicating the entire Shroud's image authentically. Fundamental physical paradoxes, such as the timing and speed constraints imposed by the distance the light must traverse without incineration, remain unsolved.

The event horizon theory:

The event horizon theory related to the image on the Shroud of Turin was proposed by Isabel Piczek, a Hungarian-trained particle physicist. According to this theory, the image represents a unique event horizon, a boundary in space-time with specialized physical properties.

Piczek explains that the Shroud's image shows characteristics of an event horizon where time and space break down to absolute zero. This event horizon divides the frontal image and the dorsal image of the body, creating an interface that blocks communication between the two sides. Unlike an event horizon around a black hole, which is tied to gravity and space-time collapse into a singularity. The Shroud's event horizon paradoxically shows no gravity but strong organizing energy, possibly due to reversed entropy, which overpowers gravity while maintaining an event horizon effect. The theory posits that when Christ's body, wrapped in the Shroud, underwent what can be interpreted as a "quantum time collapse," the two event horizons on each side of the body got so close that they merged and then disappeared, causing a freeze or collapse of time (absolute zero). This collapse recorded the image of the dead body on both sides of the Shroud in a three-dimensional, holographic-like manner. The image is negative and has a retrospective quality, meaning the image on the cloth captures the dead body at the last moment before the body left the tomb. This theory connects the image to a quantum hologram phenomenon. A singularity-like moment, akin to the creation of a universe (a Big Bang type singularity) but not resulting in a black hole. In this view, the image on the Shroud is not a simple photograph or painting but an imprint formed through a complex interaction of space-time singularities and quantum event horizons that reflect the supernatural nature of the Resurrection event. Including a collapse and subsequent phase transformation of time itself. The event horizon theory of the Shroud image suggests the image was formed by a unique quantum event involving event horizons and space-time singularities that froze the last moment of Christ's body in a kind of quantum hologram on the cloth. This event horizon is distinct from black hole horizons because it shows no gravity and involves reversed entropy and new physics beyond conventional understanding.

At first, I didn't understand the reason for this theory. It seems a bit farfetched and akin to other radiation theories but different. Later, I discovered the reasoning. The Shroud of Turin posits that the image on the Shroud was created by radiation emitted vertically from within the body wrapped in the cloth. This radiation was collimated (focused) vertically, straight up and down, rather than being emitted in all directions. This vertical emission is essential to explain why the Shroud shows clear, high-resolution images only of the front and back of the body, but no images of the sides or top of the head and had to be vertically collimated so that each point on the cloth corresponded to a single point on the surface of the body, either the front or back. This "one-to-one correspondence" prevents image blurring or confusion, which would happen if radiation was emitted randomly in all directions. No lenses existed between the body and cloth to focus radiation from all around the body onto the cloth. Without vertical collimation, the image would be blurry or missing since radiation from side points would scatter and overlap on the cloth. Because of this vertical emission, only the front and dorsal (back) images appear on the Shroud, with no side or top of the head images, matching the actual evidence on the cloth. In the context of the Shroud of Turin and the radiation theory, the term "true event horizon" has been used metaphorically to describe a unique boundary related to the image formation on the Shroud. This boundary, or "event horizon," is not the astronomical black hole event horizon but a conceptual interface dividing two regions of the Shroud image system, an upper region and a lower region.

The event horizon on the Shroud marks a critical boundary where time appears to stop and events are frozen in that moment, creating the image seen on the cloth. It represents a sort of "interface" that separates two distinct regions. Unlike typical event horizons in astrophysics associated with gravity and black holes, the Shroud's event horizon paradoxically shows no gravity but an intense energy release and a decrease in entropy that organizes the energy. This energy and the event horizon concept are used to explain the unique features of the Shroud image, including the detailed, frozen-in-time appearance and its semi-three-dimensional relief effect. The radiation involved is thought to be a highly focused burst of ultraviolet or particle radiation emitted vertically (front to back) from the body.

The event horizon concept also helps explain 2 events, the first is how time could "collapse" to zero and how the image could encode both space-like and time-like singularities, similar to phenomena in cosmology but here relating to the image and information transfer onto the Shroud. The interaction of vertical radiation emitted during this event horizon state is believed to have created the image in a focused manner on the Shroud, without blurring from side radiation, forming the sharp front and back images observed without side images. The second is the hair at the side of the face as opposed to pushed back by gravity. It also explains why there is no flattening effect on the back half of the body, due to weight, lying on a hard surface.

Thus, the "true event horizon" in this context is a theoretical boundary or interface connected to the moment of intense radiation emission from the body that resulted in the formation of the Shroud's front and back images via vertically collimated radiation. It reflects a boundary in space-time where the image's information was imprinted on the cloth in a highly ordered, energy-intensive process unlike common physical phenomena

The radiation-based image formation hypothesis on linen involves an extremely brief, intense burst of UV or VUV radiation that alters the superficial fibers chemically without heat damage, reproducing the Shroud's unique superficial and 3D imaging traits. Experimental laser studies support the feasibility of superficial discoloration but expose the enormous physical and energetic challenges to replicating the entire Shroud's image authentically. Fundamental physical distance light must traverse without incineration, remain unsolved paradoxes, such as the timing, speed and heat.

A personal journey into the mystery of the Shroud

The image on an event horizon

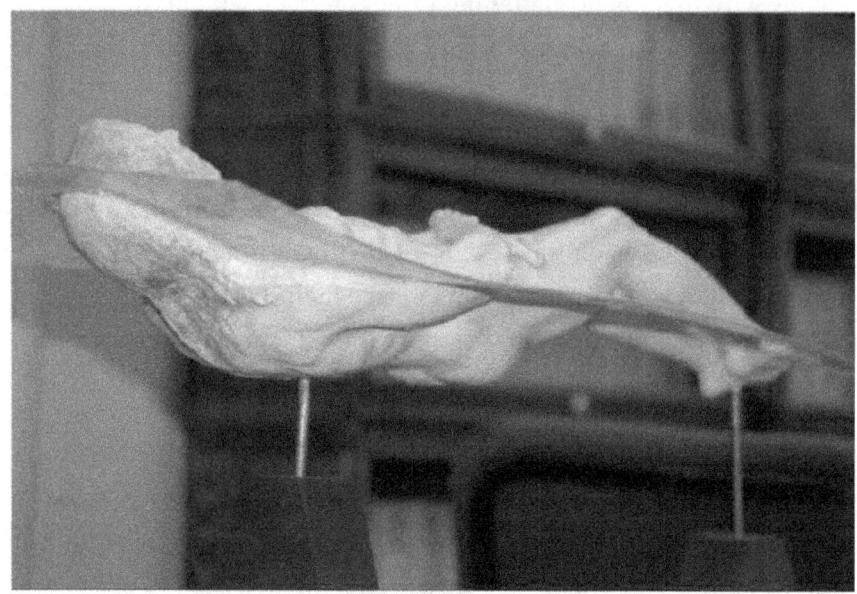

THE EVENT HORIZON OF THE SHROUD OF TURIN BY ISABEL PICZEK

Chapter 6: Artificial Intelligence
What is Artificial Intelligence?

Artificial intelligence (AI) is a branch of computer science dedicated to developing creating machines and software capable of performing tasks that traditionally required human intelligence. These tasks include learning from experience, understanding language, recognizing patterns, solving problems, reasoning, making decisions, and adapting to new information. AI systems rely on leverage algorithms, data, and computational power to simulate human cognitive functions and continuously improve their performance over time without explicit reprogramming.

In recent years, breakthroughs in machine learning particularly deep learning, and the rise of generative AI, have greatly expanded AI's role in scientific research. Today, AI is applied to data analysis, pattern recognition, predictive modeling, and problem-solving across disciplines such as biology, chemistry, physics, and the social sciences. This transformation is ushering in a new era in which AI accelerates discovery, automates experimentation, and augments human research capabilities.

AI-augmented research refers to the integration of AI into the research process to enhance productivity, accelerate discovery, and improve decision-making. Unlike simple automation, AI acts as a powerful collaborator, decoding complex datasets, predicting experimental outcomes, generating novel hypotheses, and streamlining workflows. By handling repetitive tasks such as data processing and experimental setup, AI frees researchers to focus on higher-level strategic and creative work. Studies suggest this integration can boost research productivity by 30–50% and reduce time-to-market by as much as 40% in innovation-driven fields.

In practice AI accelerates data analysis, reveals hidden patterns, and enables advanced predictive modeling and simulation, reducing reliance on costly physical experiments. For example, in drug discovery, AI expedites the identification of promising compounds, while in materials science, it predicts the properties and performance of novel materials. Beyond technical applications, AI also fosters interdisciplinary collaboration, enables real-time data analysis, and supports evidence-based decision-making through optimized resource allocation. Collectively, these capabilities are transforming research into a more efficient, innovative, and impactful endeavor.

Additionally, AI assists in predictive modeling by using historical data to forecast trends and outcomes, deepening our understanding of cause-and-effect relationships. It also aids in deciphering ancient languages, digitizing and preserving archival materials, and identifying biases embedded in historical narratives. By integrating diverse sources and cross-referencing data, AI enables a more nuanced and comprehensive understanding of the past, challenging entrenched assumptions and offering fresh interpretations.

Regarding the significance of these technological advancements in relation to the Shroud of Turin:

The integration of advanced AI and quantum computing could offer unprecedented tools for analyzing complex historical artifacts like the Shroud of Turin. Enhanced image processing, pattern recognition, and material simulations might lead to new scientific insights about its origins, composition, and authenticity, potentially resolving longstanding debates with greater precision. Advanced AI and quantum computing technologies hold significant promise for deepening our understanding of this enigmatic artifact by offering powerful new analytical capabilities:

Enhanced Image Analysis and Pattern Recognition
AI-powered neural networks and deep learning models can analyze high-resolution images of the Shroud with a level of detail and subtlety far beyond human perception. These models can detect and highlight faint patterns, textures, and features invisible to the naked eye or traditional image processing techniques. For example, AI can reveal underlying marks, bloodstains, or textural inconsistencies that provide clues about the cloth's history and formation.

Material and Chemical Composition Analysis
Quantum-enhanced AI simulations can model the molecular and chemical interactions within the fibers of the Shroud. Such analysis can uncover precise information about the linen, paint pigments (if any), or biological residues without damaging the artifact. Quantum simulations could reproduce how certain materials behave under various environmental conditions over centuries, helping researchers understand aging processes or artificial alterations.

Carbon Dating and Chronology Verification
While radiocarbon dating has been controversial due to sampling limitations and potential contamination, AI algorithms optimized by quantum computing could better calibrate dating data by integrating and analyzing broader environmental and chemical variables. This may improve the precision and reliability of determining the cloth's age.

Reconstruction of Historical Context

AI models trained on extensive historical, artistic, and textile data could help reconstruct the manufacturing techniques and cultural context of the Shroud's origin. By comparing the Shroud's characteristics with data from other ancient textiles, AI could provide insights into its geographic and temporal background.

Simulation of Image Formation Mechanisms

One of the most debated questions is how the image on the Shroud was created. Quantum AI could simulate multiple hypotheses, such as chemical reactions, radiation effects, or artistic techniques at an atomic level. Testing which process is most consistent with observed data. These simulations could provide scientific validation or refutation of various theories about the image's formation.

Preservation and Authentication Methods

AI-driven monitoring systems could be used to ensure optimal preservation conditions for the Shroud, predicting environmental impacts and degradation risks with high accuracy. Furthermore, quantum-enhanced cryptographic techniques could secure and authenticate digital data related to the Shroud's studies, ensuring integrity and trustworthiness of research findings.

The convergence of AI and quantum computing represents a transformative leap in the scientific study of the Shroud of Turin. These technologies could help answer perplexing questions about its origin, authenticity, and the nature of its image while preserving this priceless artifact for future generations. The resolution of these mysteries using cutting-edge technology would not only deepen our historical and religious understanding but also showcase the profound potential of AI and quantum advancements in cultural heritage research.

The Man of the Shroud facial and physical reconstruction by Artificial Intelligence created from the Shroud of Turin. Is this the face of Jesus Christ?

Facial Reconstruction of a Crucified Man using AI tools, researchers recreated a lifelike face from the Shroud's facial imprint, depicting a man with shoulder-length hair, a beard, deep-set eyes, (often rendered as blue), and wounds on his chest and body indicative of torture and death. The AI-enhanced images show closed eyes, a slightly parted mouth, and signs of recent crucifixion (e.g. scourging marks), aligning with biblical descriptions of Jesus. This has gone viral, inspiring discussions on the "real" face of Christ. While not proving identity, the reconstruction concludes the image is of a real human who suffered extreme trauma, not an artistic invention.

Chapter 7: Who is it?

There is historical correspondence to crucifixion accounts for example, the wounds shown on the Shroud align closely with the Gospel descriptions: scourging, crown of thorns, pierced side, wrist/foot nailing. The image also portrays crucifixion in a manner consistent with Roman execution practices of the 1st century, but not well known in medieval Europe. There is anatomical & medical accuracy in that forensic experts have noted that the wounds, blood flows, and body proportions are consistent with real human physiology and trauma. Details like the blood serum separation (halo effect) weren't understood until modern hematology.

The nature of the Image is complicated; the image is not painted; there are no brushstrokes or pigment layers. Microscopic studies show the image is only on the very top fibrils of the linen threads, like a surface discoloration. It behaves like a photographic negative (first discovered in 1898 by Secondo Pia), which seems beyond medieval artistry Pollen & Material Evidence. Pollen grains and dust unique to the Middle East (especially Jerusalem area plants) were reportedly found on the cloth. Some textile experts note that the herringbone weave and stitching style could be consistent with 1st-century cloth from the Eastern Mediterranean. Although gaps exist, some argue the Shroud can be traced back through Constantinople (the "Image of Edessa" or Mandylion) and even earlier.

Advanced AI and forensic reconstructions based on the Shrouds image depict a Middle Eastern man approximately 5'11" tall, weighing about 175 pounds, and possessing a strong, well-conditioned physique, attributes consistent with someone

A personal journey into the mystery of the Shroud

accustomed to extensive daily walking while preaching. He appears to be between 30 and 35 years old, with Semitic features including long hair and a beard. This portrayal closely aligns with traditional representations, notably the 6th-century Christ Pantocrator icon at St. Catherine's Monastery, one of the oldest Byzantine images of Jesus. These features contrast sharply with skeptic claims of European traits but corresponding 1st century Jewish norms.

The 6th-century Christ Pantocrator icon at St. Catherine's Monastery

This raises a compelling question: if the Shroud of Turin does not depict Jesus of Nazareth as described in the Bible, then who could it represent? The Romans, and the Persians before them, carried out thousands of crucifixions. Yet none of those known executions involved a crown of thorns or the distinctive details surrounding Jesus's death. If the Shroud is a medieval forgery created with actual human blood, both pre- and post-mortem, would that suggest that someone was crucified in a manner precisely replicating the biblical accounts? The man of the Shroud appears crowned with thorns, an image rarely, if ever pictured as a cap, pierced by a Roman lance, and left with unbroken legs. This combination of elements indicates not a typical crucifixion, but one strikingly aligned with the Gospel narratives.

The burial cloth itself raises further questions. The high-quality linen is unusual for the interment of a crucified criminal, if such individuals were buried at all. Some researchers have claimed that the word "Nazarene" appears in Aramaic on the Shroud, however, convincing evidence is lacking. A careful study concluded that the supposed inscriptions contain too many linguistic and paleographic errors to be considered reliable. Jewish burial customs did not identify the body in a shroud. The name was on an ossuary which was a bone box where the remains were placed later. Scholars caution that patterns identified as writing may simply be stains, folds, or random marks. As such, there is no scholarly consensus regarding authentic inscriptions on the cloth. While it has been argued that inscribing a name on a burial cloth aligns with certain Jewish customs, placing it near the head for identification, no definitive proof supports that this was done here.

Similarly, claims that coins from the era of Pontius Pilate were placed over the eyes of the man of the Shroud remain unverified. Although two circular shapes appear near the eyes in certain photographs, they cannot be reliably identified as coins. Many such interpretations stem from light artifacts or natural creases in the cloth. The most comprehensive scientific investigation, the STURP study of 1978, did not confirm any coin impressions. While they documented the Shroud's many unique features, they found no high-confidence evidence of embedded objects. Further, it does not make sense that pagan coins would be used in a Jewish burial. This is actually a Pagan custom.

In my own study of the images, two details stood out. First, the hair on the Shroud falls straight alongside the face, an unlikely occurrence for a supine body, where gravity would normally pull the hair backward. Second, the image on the reverse shows rounded buttocks instead of the flattened appearance expected if the body were lying on a hard surface such as a stone slab. Initially, I considered this observation original, until I encountered it in Dr. Gilbert Lavoie's insightful book The Shroud of Jesus, which I highly recommend for its careful and detailed analysis.

The biblical references also invite reexamination. The Gospels describe Jesus's body being wrapped in linen: sindon ("fine linen") in Mark 15:46, and othonia ("linen wrappings") in Luke 24:12 and John 20:5–7, with John adding the detail of a separate sudarium covering the face. When John 20:8 records that the disciple "saw and believed," I do not interpret this as seeing an image imprinted on the cloth. Rather, he likely saw the undisturbed wrappings and the separate folded face cloth in place. The apostle understood that no one would unwrap a decomposing body, especially after three days, in order to steal it. As shown in the story of Lazarus, where Martha warned Jesus of the stench after only four days, it would have been unthinkable for grave robbers to unwrap such a body to remove it. Thus, the simplest conclusion that John could draw was that Jesus himself had risen and left the wrappings behind.

Additional physical details further link the Shroud to the crucifixion described in the Gospels. The inward-folded thumbs point to nail placement in the wrists rather than the palms. The bruising on one shoulder is consistent with carrying a heavy wooden beam. The dumbbell-shaped wounds align with scourging by a Roman flagrum. Collectively, these elements harmonize with historical and biblical accounts in a strikingly coherent way.

Even after rigorous scrutiny with modern technology, the Shroud still defies classification as medieval artwork or forgery. Applying Occam's Razor, the principle that the simplest explanation requiring the fewest assumptions is usually correct, the most reasonable conclusion is that the Man of the Shroud is indeed Jesus of Nazareth. Attempts to replicate it scientifically have failed, and the improbability of its being anyone else is, quite literally, astronomical.

Chapter 8: How and why was it done?

Attempts to replicate the Shroud have repeatedly failed. In 2022, British filmmaker David Rolfe offered £1 million to anyone who could successfully duplicate the Shroud. Despite many efforts, no one has claimed the prize. Some attempts border on the absurd, ignoring established research. An example being the most recent, by Brazilian 3D artist and researcher Cicero Moraes, published October 29, 2024, and later covered by sensationalist media in 2025. Moraes used advanced 3D modeling to digitally drape cloth over a human body and a shallow relief sculpture. He concluded the Shrouds image more closely resembles fabric pressed onto a low-relief sculpture than a real body, based on what he called the "Agamemnon Mask effect," where fabric distorts when draped over a real human form. In contrast, simulated cloth over a relief produces an image matching the Shroud more closely, leading Moraes to propose it is medieval Christian art rather than a genuine burial cloth. However, experts and institutions in Shroud research have widely criticized Moraes's work for multiple reasons:

Methodological superficiality: His digital approach lacks integration of crucial physical and chemical analyses, such as blood flow patterns, textile fiber examination, and chemical composition.

Ignoring historical and scientific context: Decades of established research, including the 1970s Shroud of Turin Research Project (STURP), have excluded image formation by base- relief or pigments, showing the image is a faint oxidation of cellulose, not paint or burn, something Moraes's model does not replicate.

Incomplete and inaccurate modeling: The digital simulation omits the Shrouds dorsal image and misrepresents anatomical posture, even reversing hand and foot positioning for convenience.

No physical experimentation: Moraes's research is purely virtual and lacks testing with actual linen or materials. While Moraes offers valuable digital visualization, his research is methodologically weak, historically uninformed, and incomplete. It has not altered the broader scientific consensus nor added substantive new insights beyond long-standing Shroud research. While Moraes' 3D modeling strengthens the bas-relief case by explaining proportional anatomy without full-body distortions, the criticisms are valid, it doesn't fully reconcile with STURP's chemical/physical data or the image's non-contact 3D projection. The medieval dating (C14: 1260–1390 AD) and historical records (e.g., 1389 forgery claim) still tilt toward artistic origin, but anomalies like pollen and WAXS keep authenticity debates alive. No theory perfectly replicates all properties yet, and further testing (e.g., new C14 on uncontaminated areas) is needed. When all elements are considered, radiation fits the 3D data better.

A personal journey into the mystery of the Shroud

Comparison

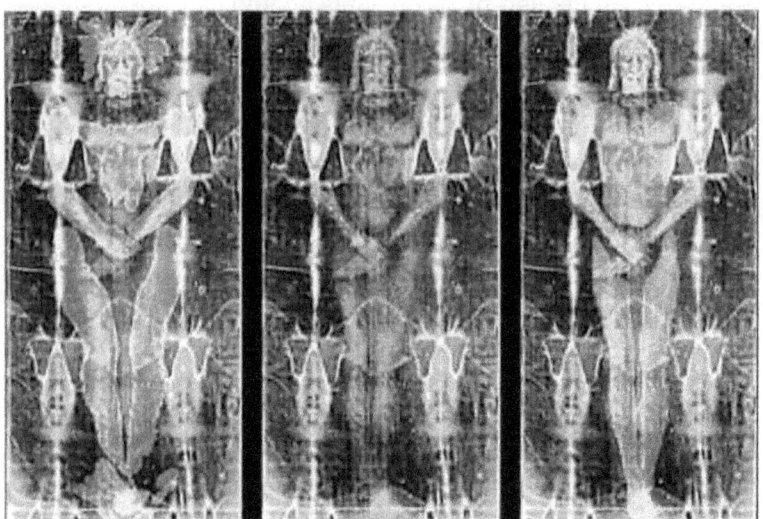

Agamemnon Mask   Actual Shroud   Cicero Moraes

More than a relic, the Shroud appears designed to endure 2,000 years, carrying a message to modern humanity akin to that given to the Apostle Thomas after the resurrection: an invitation to encounter truth through tangible evidence. Recent analyses of the Shroud using digital tools face significant limitations. Current software cannot rigorously simulate fabric-body or fabric-sculpture interactions, undermining claims about the image's formation. The theory that the Shroud's image resembles an orthogonal projection or bas-relief imprint is not new, having been debated for over a century. Leading authorities, including the International Center of Sindonology and Turin's archbishop, urge caution, criticizing media-driven studies for lacking scientific depth. These studies often overlook complex features, such as Middle Eastern pollen, traces of aloe, and myrrh, and human blood stains consistent with crucifixion wounds, which suggest a purpose beyond mere artifact. Why do discredited theories about the Shroud persist in academic journals? The answer reflects a broader trend in journalism over the past 10–15 years, where the pursuit of truth has often been eclipsed by the quest for profit, or "clicks." Sensational headlines prioritize attention over accuracy, reducing the Shroud's profound mystery to a media spectacle. Yet, this distortion may inadvertently amplify its intended message, drawing modern eyes to a 2,000-year-old enigma.

As of 2025, the Shroud remains polarizing, viewed by some as a medieval icon akin to Michelangelo's Pietà, deeply meaningful and beautiful to believers, yet dismissed by skeptics as art. This divide is striking among scientists, who demand extraordinary evidence for the Shroud's authenticity but readily accept theories like the Big Bang without similar scrutiny. The James Webb Space Telescope's recent findings, which challenge cosmological models, remind us that scientific certainty is fleeting. The Shroud, however, seems crafted to endure such shifts, its image and traces defying explanation, much like the wounds Christ showed Thomas to affirm his resurrection. Is the Shroud actually presenting itself to the unbelievers of the 21st century. The people of this century did not have the advantage of meeting and witnessing the works of Jesus. They are asked to believe although they have not seen. Jesus himself said blessed are those who believe who have not seen. That seems to indicate he knew there would be others like Thomas who said unless I put my hand in the wounds I will not believe he has risen. Could the Shroud be a time capsule for the 21st century containing a message from Jesus himself?

Unlike artifacts with clear provenance, such as King Tutankhamen's tomb, which remained undisturbed for millennia, the Shroud has traveled across countries for 2,000 years, sometimes for protection, to spread its message. This journey mirrors the early Christian mission to bear witness, suggesting the Shroud was meant to endure as a testament. The Catholic Church, its custodian since King Umberto II's bequest in 1983, remains silent on its authenticity. The Church's official stance has been cautious and measured. While early popes like Julius II in the early 16th century permitted public veneration of the Shroud as if authentic, the Church never made a definitive pronouncement on its authenticity. Instead, it allowed the faithful to venerate it and come to their own conclusions. The Catholic faith, it emphasizes, does not depend on the Shroud's authenticity but on the testimony of the apostles about Jesus's resurrection.

In the 20th and 21st centuries, Popes John Paul II, Benedict XVI, and Pope Francis have all recognized the Shroud as a powerful religious symbol and "a mirror of the Gospel," an "icon" of the suffering of Christ, and a focus for devotion. The Church also acknowledging that scientific questions about its origin remain unresolved and that the Church leaves the matter of authenticity to scientific investigation and the personal faith of individuals. The Shroud thus holds a revered place within the Catholic Church as a significant religious relic and object of devotion, but the Church maintains a stance of non-commitment to its authenticity, focusing instead on its spiritual meaning. The cloth's history reflects a complex narrative of religious faith, political history, and ongoing scientific scrutiny. The 1988 carbon-dating results, suggesting a medieval origin, were later questioned due to potential contamination, yet the Church's reticence aligns with the Shroud's subtle purpose: to invite contemplation, not demand proclamation.

Skepticism about the Shroud dates back centuries. In the 14th century, Bishop Pierre d'Arcis of Troyes objected to its exhibition near his cathedral, citing an alleged artist's confession of forgery reported by his predecessor. Was this objection driven by theological concern or competition for pilgrims? The historical context suggests the Shroud's true nature was elusive, as premodern societies lacked the technology to analyze its unique properties. I propose this was by design: the Shroud was created to be fully understood only in an age of advanced science, delivering its message to a skeptical, modern world, much as Christ's wounds convinced Thomas. A time capsule that when opened provides the kind of proof that the apostles were allowed to see but the people of the 21st century can only imagine. I began my inquiry as a skeptic with doubts as firm as that of Barrie Schwortz, the photographer, from the 1978 Shroud of Turin Research Project. Though raised in the rhythms and symbols of Catholic tradition, the Shroud to me, was little more than another devotional object, like the Stations of the Cross that I walked as a child; each scene etched into ritual and meaning but abstract from day-to-day life. The 1988 carbon-14 dating, with its confident verdict of "medieval forgery," seemed to confirm my indifference. The matter was settled, or so I thought. Yet something, call it curiosity, or perhaps the quiet pull of mystery, drew me back.

When I finally lingered over the Shroud's details, the spectral image, the rivulets of blood, the whisper of pollen grains from far-off lands, I began to feel I was in the presence of something meant to survive the centuries. Not simply preserved, but prepared, deliberately fashioned to outlast empires, cultures, and creeds. Until the day when it could confront an age like ours, where faith and technology watch each other with wary eyes. Its history is like a missing thread in a tapestry: the Shroud appears without warning in one place, vanishes for generations, reemerges elsewhere, intact, defiant, refusing to be forgotten. In this pattern, I heard an echo of the apostle Thomas, invited to put his hand into Christ's wounds, a call not to blind belief, but to touch, to examine, and in doing so, to wrestle with the possibility of truth.

I am not what one would call devout, yet, the more I studied the Shroud, the more this linen relic unsettled me. It did not speak in proclamations; it spoke like an ancient whisper to the soul. See, touch, believe. The Catholic Church, its custodian since 1983, remains largely silent. Perhaps wisely so. For the Shroud's strength may lie not in declaration, but in provocation: an unvoiced challenge laid across the centuries, daring us to seek beyond the easy answers. If the Shroud has a message or messages, then what is it saying? Many believers skip to the conclusion that the Shroud is proof of the Resurrection. They insist, its unrepeatable image is the signature of a supernatural act. Science, they argue, has failed to recreate it even with twenty-first century technology; therefore, it must be divine. The Shroud has order and precision detail that suggests authorship. Yet my mind returns to an older truth: extraordinary claims require extraordinary evidence, and science has not yet handed us proof of a miracle. However, science must follow the facts and in the absence of scientific explanation the obvious must be true.

Others cling to the "ingenious forgery" theory with equal certainty; despite the growing list of scientific puzzles, it leaves unresolved. In time, I realized I had to read the Shroud differently. Jesus seldom spoke in absolutes; He spoke in parables, stories that demanded engagement and reflection. If He left us a message or messages woven in cloth, I doubt He intended it to be a simple proof for the Resurrection. No, the Shroud does not prove. It invites, it beckons us to return, over and over, to its haunting image from head to toe. It asks us, to attend to its silence as intently as its signs, and to wonder, perhaps against our will, what truth might be hidden there, waiting for the one who looks long enough. At this point, I wondered if the message is the same for each of, us or does it say different things to different people. Right now, my concern is what is it saying to me. In order to determine that I had to return to the cloth in detail and reviewed what I was seeing.

The Shroud of Turin depicts a full-body image of a man with various wounds consistent with historical accounts of crucifixion and torture. The benefit derived from the 3-dimensional image is that more accurately displays the content that might not be available from a 2-dimensional image.

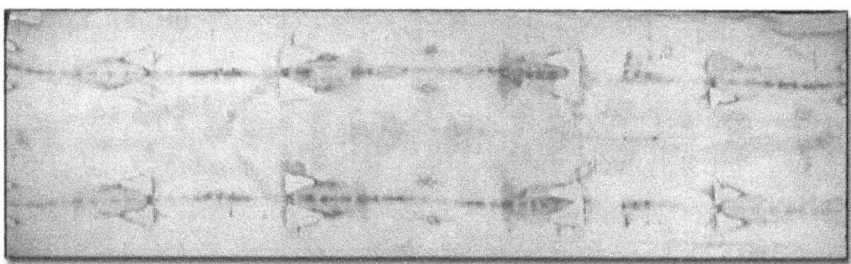

The Shroud of Turin ©1978 Barrie M. Schwortz

When the Shroud is on display, we glimpse a faint barely visible image on the cloth. What exactly are we looking at? It appears to be a linen cloth bearing barely discernible markings that many identify as the image of a crucified man. This is essentially how early observers perceived it. To the uninitiated, it could seem like a

A personal journey into the mystery of the Shroud

stained burial cloth, perhaps marked by blood or an ointment used in the burial process. Yet because it concerns the cloth of Jesus, it had to be preserved. The Bible quotes the Gospel of John, chapter 20, verse 8. After Peter and "the other disciple" (traditionally understood to be John) arrived at Jesus' tomb, it says: "Then the other disciple, who had reached the tomb first, also went in. He saw and believed." (John 20:8, various translations). There are no further direct quotes from the disciple at this point; the text simply states that upon entering the tomb and seeing the linen cloths, "He saw and believed," indicating his faith in Jesus' resurrection. This phrase is often interpreted as referring to the image on the Shroud. But was he actually speaking about the image or the empty tomb? When Mary Magdalene arrived early that morning, while it was still dark, she noticed the stone had been rolled away from the tomb entrance. Shocked and distressed, she ran to tell Simon Peter, and the other disciple that someone had taken the Lord's body, and she did not know where it had been laid. The image on the Shroud was not clear enough to be recognized as a miracle in the first century. In fact, the closer one looks, the more the details seem to fade. To first-century observers, the Shroud was undoubtedly a sacred relic. It is unlikely that the apostles or others close to Jesus examined the burial cloth closely; its mere presence was enough to regard it as holy. The key question is whether those early witnesses truly understood what they had. After all, the Shroud does not easily convey its message by first-century standards. Today, modern technology alters our perception. For instance, on a smart phone, you can adjust display settings or invert colors to reveal different details of the same image. In the 21st century, it is relatively easy to discern the peculiarities of the Shroud, though interpretations of what these peculiarities mean remain highly debated.

Chapter 9: Technology Advances

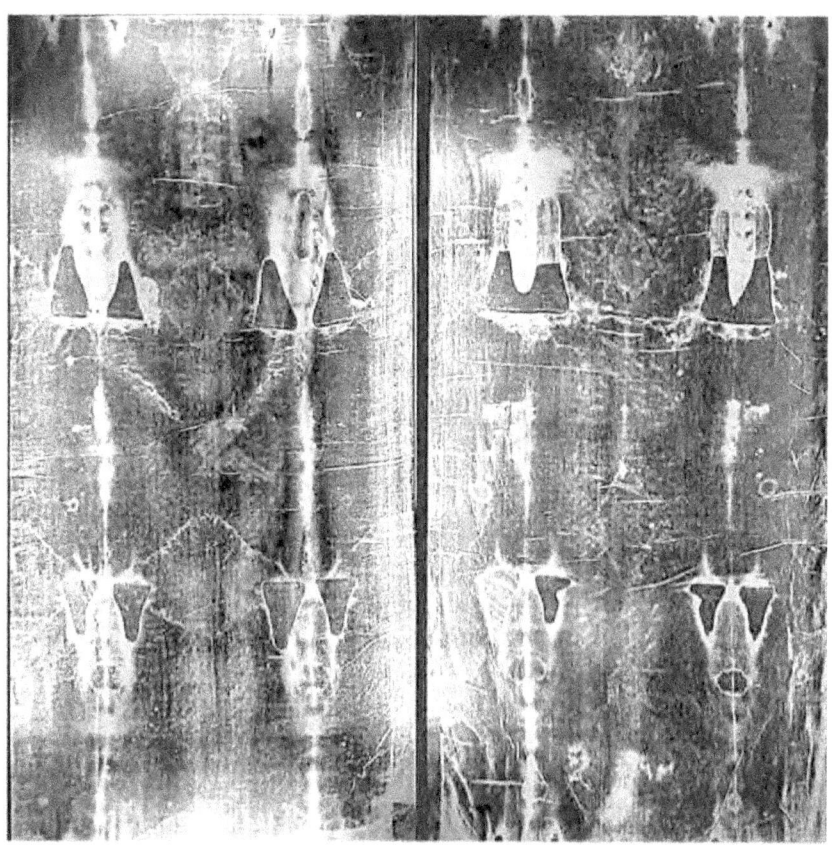

The Shroud of Turin ©1978 Barrie M. Schwortz

This picture has considerably more detail but is it enough to convey a message? I am not sure, but it was enough to kick off a lot of investigation over a long period of time.

A personal journey into the mystery of the Shroud

Moving forward again:

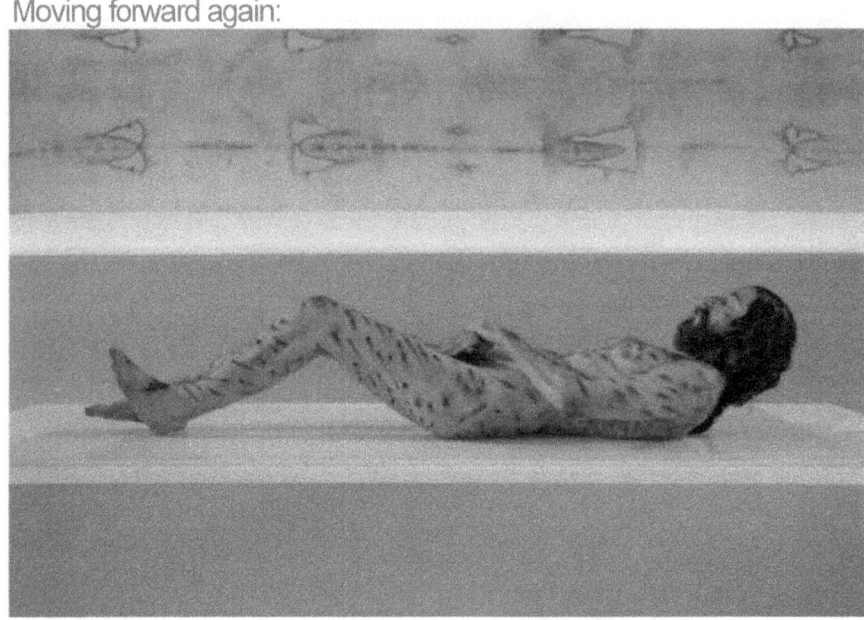

We now have a 3-dimensional model of the image from the Shroud. Note the magnitude of the wounds.

The image of a man brutally beaten confronts us, but have we truly grasped its message? To understand its significance, we must consider the purpose behind this act. Jesus' ultimate mission was to sacrifice himself for humanity's salvation. Unlike His parables, which taught lessons of love, behavior, and redemption, this was the definitive act, the ultimate message. The details of what we see on the reconstructed image are as follows:

Scourge/flagellation marks: Total of 372 visible marks (159 on the front, 213 on the back), caused by a Roman flagrum (whip with multiple thongs ending in dumbbell-shaped weights or bone/metal fragments). These are distributed across multiple body areas, with more on the back. Each "lash" likely produced 2-3 marks, suggesting approximately 120-180 lashes total. Marks are categorized into types: Type 1 (dumbbell-shaped, ~115 visible), Type 2 (striped bands, ~170 visible), and Type 3 (fan-shaped, <15, mostly on legs/calves).

Other wounds: Specific counts for nail wounds (4 total punctures), side wound (1), and abrasions/swelling where quantified.

Where exact distribution per area is not specified in sources, approximations are noted based on descriptions (e.g., denser on back and legs). Total wounds exceed 400 when including all types. The list focuses on what is directly observable from bloodstains, imprints, and injuries.

Head:

Puncture wounds from a crown of thorns: Over 50 puncture wounds encircling the skull, caused by sharp thorns (e.g., from ziziphus jujuba). Bloodstains include one median flow (resembling "3" in negative or epsilon/omega), two lateral flows on the forehead, and clots on the forehead, temples, neck, scalp, and hair. Additional arterial/venous hemorrhages peripherally on the skull. At least 1 scourge mark on the dorsal head image, and possibly 1 on the right eye (vertical mark).

Facial swelling and trauma: Swelling in the forehead, superciliary arches, mid-frontal area, right eyebrow (partially closing the eye), and left nasal dorsum (deviated nose from fracture). Large triangular contusion on the right cheek. Bruised chin, lips, mustache, chin, and beard with blood clots; streams of blood mixed with saliva/pulmonary edema from the mouth and nostrils. Missing hair patches in the beard (as if pulled out).

Total estimated for area: ~50-60 (primarily thorn punctures, plus 1-2 scourge marks and facial contusions).

Shoulders and Upper Back:

Abrasions and bruises: Marks on the right and left shoulders, shoulder blades, and nape of neck from contact with a heavy, angular object (e.g., patibulum crossbeam). Includes excoriations and possible shoulder dislocation from crucifixion positioning.

Scourge marks: Part of the 213 back marks; denser in this area, with overlapping Type 1 and Type 2 marks (dumbbell and striped). Specific count not isolated, but estimated ~40-60 based on distribution (crowded on upper back).

Total estimated for area: ~40-60 (abrasions not quantified, scourge subset).

Torso (Front and Back):

Scourge marks: Part of the total 372 (159 front including chest/abdomen; 213 back including buttocks). Front: Type 1 scarce, Type 2 abundant with overlapping; back: Type 1 and Type 2 crowded, with remarkable bleeding in some spots. Estimated ~100-150 total for torso (more on back, ~80-100; front ~40-50).

Side wound: 1 oval-shaped puncture on the right side (appearing left in negative), ~2.25 inches wide and 6 inches long, between the 5th and 6th ribs. Caused by a Roman lance post-mortem, piercing the pleura, pericardium, and right atrium; blood and watery fluid (plasma/pleural effusion) flowed in multiple directions (vertical, 45°, horizontal). Partially obscured by a 1532 patch; exit hole noted on left back below scapula.

Other: Blood clots in gluteal area (back); earthy material mixed with blood.

Total estimated for area: ~101-151 (scourge + 1 side wound).

Arms and Forearms:

Blood flows from wrist wounds: Traces on forearms consistent with arms extended during crucifixion; blood off the right elbow.

Scourge marks: Present on forearms (Type 1 noted); part of front/back totals, but specific count low (~10-20 estimated).

Total estimated for area: ~10-20 (primarily scourge, plus blood flows not counted as separate wounds).

Hands and Wrists

Nail wounds: 2 punctures (1 per wrist), through Destot's space (between carpal bones), damaging the median nerve and causing thumb contraction (thumbs hidden, only 4 fingers visible). Blood clots with fibrin; pre-mortem and post-mortem flows, plus serum leaks under UV.

Legs (Thighs and Calves)

Scourge marks: Continuation from torso; part of 372 total (front legs ~50-70 of 159; back legs ~60-80 of 213). Type 1 and Type 2 equally represented on calves; Type 3 (<15 total) on thighs/calves/near ankles. Overlapping and cylindrical deformation on lower legs.

Knee injuries: Numerous excoriations (right knee: multiple sizes with substance loss; left: less extensive); swelling suggesting possible kneecap fracture from falls.

Total estimated for area: ~120-170 (scourge + knee excoriations; scourge denser here, especially back).

Feet:

Nail wounds: 2 punctures (1 per foot); right foot wound on metatarsal bones (between 2nd/3rd cuneiform or sinus tarsi); left foot possibly on top of right, with entry at heel/central part. Blood flows on top/bottom of feet; right foot full imprint with middle stain, left heel profuse with blood and handler fingerprints.

Scourge marks: Included in leg totals; Type 3 near ankles (~5-10 estimated).

Total estimated for area: ~7-12 (2 nail + subset of scourge).

We look to Artificial Intelligence (AI)

A 2025 study published in the International Journal of Archaeology applied advanced AI-driven pattern recognition and image processing techniques to the Shroud. Researchers analyzed both visible light and ultraviolet-induced fluorescence images, converting them to the CIE Lab color space to enhance analysis. The results demonstrate that the primary information content lies in the image intensity, and differentiation of this intensity reveals clear three-dimensional properties in the image. AI discovered via information obtained via a pixel-by-pixel scan of the Shroud too detailed for the human eye. The results were startling; they included the mathematical accuracy of the human figure both in proportion and physical dimension. Well beyond what an artist could achieve. The blood is real and the wounds and blood flow are consistent with the biblical text. This AI-based analysis supports the theory that radiation, and possibly several types, may have contributed to the image formation. Several other examinations have produced intriguing findings about the Shroud's properties.

Hidden Geometric Patterns:

Advanced image processing and pattern recognition algorithms uncovered a faint, structured, repeating geometry embedded within the Shroud, especially around the face and chest areas. This structure appeared across multiple layers of analysis, including ultraviolet fluorescence, thermal imaging, and high-contrast filters, suggesting the pattern was not random, nor the result of fabric folds, brushwork, or natural processes. The geometric symmetry was consistent and appeared mathematically derived, leading some scientists to describe its appearance as "engineered". We discussed the discovery of three, dimensional properties however, with AI-assisted differentiation of image intensity and other computational imaging techniques demonstrated that the Shroud's image encodes three-dimensional information, not typical of regular flat images. This finding reinforces previous observations that suggested the image is not simply a flat painting or print, but carries depth-valued data.

AI analysis of both visible light and fluorescence images suggested that the "image intensity" (the light-dark values that make up the face and details on the Shroud) is primarily responsible for the Shroud's mysterious visual imprint. The study noted that the image formation mechanism could be compatible with certain types of radiation exposure, though it did not conclusively identify a specific physical process. Using high-resolution scans, generative AI platforms attempted to reconstruct the physical appearance of the man imprinted on the cloth. The resulting image depicted a rugged middle eastern man with features that matched forensic reconstructions of first-century Jewish males and wounds consistent with Roman crucifixion practices, not stylized religious art. Anthropologists commented on the striking resemblance between the AI-generated face and what scholars expect for a person from that time and place. Further analysis using generative AI revealed anomalies or "encoded" visual signatures, features not normally visible to unaided human observers and not explained by known artistic or physical methods. AI using advanced detection and analysis of microscopic image features, allowing scientists to observe and quantify characteristics that are often too subtle or complex for manual inspection. especially deep learning models, can identify and segment cells, organelles, and other microscopic objects from background noise. These models learn to classify each pixel, facilitating counting, measurement, shape analysis, and intensity/texture characterization with expert-level speed and precision. AI analysis discovered that the image formation likely involved radiation formation or an intense energy burst. AI pattern recognition and image processing techniques, applied to visible light and ultraviolet-induced fluorescence (UVIF) images, concluded that the Shroud's image was not created by traditional methods like painting, pigments, or direct body contact. Instead, the discoloration affects only the topmost fibers (a precision unachievable by known artistic techniques), with no brush strokes or pigment particles detected.

Principal Component Analysis (PCA) showed that image intensity captures nearly all meaningful information (over 96-98%), and variations in UVIF intensity suggest molecular changes in the linen, such as altered bonding, consistent with radiation effects. This supports hypotheses of image formation via UV radiation, corona discharge, neutron radiation, gamma radiation, or beta-radiation. AI detected mathematical consistency and symmetry in the image that doesn't match human-made artifacts, implying a non- natural process like a "plasma event" or energy burst. These conclusions align with experimental studies on linen fluorescence under radiation, but further non-destructive testing is recommended to identify the exact mechanism. AI also discovered hidden patterns and 3D Properties with uncovered structured, repeating geometries and hidden patterns across multiple imaging layers (e.g., ultraviolet, thermal, and high-contrast filters), particularly around the face and chest. These patterns exhibit depth changes mimicking 3D relief, as if the image encodes topographic data. Image differentiation (e.g., using Sobel operators) on negative versions of the Shroud confirmed its three-dimensional qualities, similar to results from analog tools like the VP-8 Image Analyzer but with greater precision.

The findings suggest the image framework has no clear "builder" and defies known technologies, raising questions about lost ancient methods or processes beyond normal human experience. This has shocked researchers, not by providing definitive answers, but by challenging historical and scientific understanding. While not proving identity, the reconstruction concludes the image is of a real human who suffered extreme trauma, not an artistic invention.

The AI analysis of blood particles and stains (from July 2024 studies) found evidence of severe trauma, including scourging, crown of thorns, and crucifixion wounds, matching historical accounts. The blood shows properties like high bilirubin levels, suggesting stress and dehydration. This reinforces conclusions that the Shroud wrapped a real victim of Roman execution, with blood flow patterns indicating the body was in a vertical position before horizontal. After reviewing these findings, I was convinced this is not only the burial Shroud of Jesus Christ, but proof of a resurrection event. I recognized that science does not have its extraordinary evidence yet, however I am convinced AI will eventually provide the extraordinary evidence. I am also not attempting to replace faith with mathematical probability. However, I must acknowledge that AI is programed to take in all of the data and make comparisons that humans simply cannot see.

Image Formation Radiation or an Intense Energy Burst

AI pattern recognition and image processing techniques, applied to visible light and ultraviolet-induced fluorescence (UVIF) images, concluded that the Shroud's image was not created by traditional methods like painting, pigments, or direct body contact. Instead, the discoloration affects only the topmost fibers (a precision unachievable by known artistic techniques), with no brush strokes or pigment particles detected. Principal Component Analysis (PCA) showed that image intensity captures nearly all meaningful information (over 96-98%), and variations in UVIF intensity suggest molecular changes in the linen, such as altered bonding, consistent with radiation effects.

This supports hypotheses of image formation via UV radiation, corona discharge, neutron radiation, gamma radiation, or beta-radiation from blood. AI detected mathematical consistency and symmetry in the image that doesn't match human-made artifacts, implying a non-natural process like a "plasma event" or energy burst. These conclusions align with experimental studies on linen fluorescence under radiation, but further non-destructive testing is recommended.

Hidden Patterns and 3D Properties Revealed

AI analysis is often paired with non-AI methods such as Wide-Angle X-ray Scattering (WAXS), which dated the linen to approximately 2,000 years ago, placing it in the first century A.D. (roughly A.D. 55–74) and thus compatible with the era of Jesus. This result challenges the 1988 radiocarbon dating tests, which suggested a medieval origin (1260–1390 CE). However, the WAXS method assumes stable storage conditions, and some researchers have criticized it for potential unreliability. Certain AI-driven Claims, such as interpretations implying "resurrection physics" tend to be speculative and untestable, often appearing in sensationalized media rather than peer-reviewed studies. Still, AI analysis has highlighted intriguing details that support the possibility of an ancient, radiation-formed image of a crucified man. To date, however, there is no scientific consensus on the Shroud's authenticity. Notably, the Catholic Church maintains no official position, instead encouraging further research.

Currently, the most widely supported scientific hypothesis is that the image originated from a brief, intense burst of ultraviolet (UV) radiation, possibly in the vacuum ultraviolet range, emitted from the body that was wrapped in the cloth. This conclusion comes through a process of elimination: alternative theories, such as chemical reactions, vapors, heat transfer, painting, or direct scorching—cannot explain key features of the image. For example, the discoloration is confined to the outermost linen fibers, without penetrating deeper into the weave or causing burn marks. Radiation theory also accounts for the image's distinct characteristics. The Shroud shows a precise, anatomically consistent, three-dimensional negative of both the front and back of a body, even in areas where the cloth did not touch the skin, such as where the linen lay an inch or more away. This suggests a non-contact mechanism. Moreover, the image contains qualities reminiscent of an X-ray, revealing underlying anatomical details. Laboratory experiments with lasers and ultraviolet light have demonstrated that mechanisms involving high-energy photons can reproduce effects similar to those seen on the Shroud. Yet, no known natural process in physics fully accounts for how such a radiation burst could have occurred. Looking toward the future, some speculate that breakthroughs in artificial intelligence and quantum computing may eventually provide answers. It is conceivable that, within the next decade, AI at a superintelligent level could uncover hidden patterns, messages, or data embedded in the Shroud that current science has yet to recognize

Chapter 10: My conclusions

After taking a deep dive into Shroud details, I have provided my opinions as to each segment of the Shroud journey. For me, studying the Shroud has been nothing short of transformative. Over the centuries, the Shroud's meaning has shifted from a first-century burial cloth to a medieval relic, and now to the focus of modern scientific inquiry. With each new advance in technology, more of its mysteries are revealed. My own exploration led to what I can only describe as a personal "message." Skeptics would dismiss this as wishful thinking, shaped by my Catholic background, and there is some truth in that. We are all products of our environment. But my own environment was a far cry from one that nurtured candidates for the seminary. Growing up the Bronx, New York and a career on Wall Street was not the ideal training ground for a young Christian youth. My true wish is that everyone who reads this will take it upon themselves to look into the Shroud and come to their own experience. I have never felt a sense of peace like I do today.

One detail in particular left a mark. In some places, the Shroud rests more than an inch away from the body. If radiation formed the image, how fast would it need to act? At the speed of light, ultraviolet radiation would cross 1.5 inches in just 0.127 nanoseconds. But to avoid vaporizing the cloth, the burst would have had to last no longer than about one-fortieth of a nanosecond. Current physics cannot account for such a phenomenon. When I realized this, it left me with an unexpected and unsettling sense of fear. I remember one morning, at breakfast, sharing this feeling with my wife. She looked at me curiously and asked, "Why fear?" I struggled for words. The truth was that I had long considered myself a cultural Catholic, happy to celebrate Christmas with Santa Claus and Easter with the Bunny while keeping the deeper meaning of faith at arm's length. But now, after the Shroud project, the ideas of God and Christ no longer felt distant or abstract. They had become immediate, real, and, frankly, frightening. Along the way I came upon a verse in Proverbs 9:10: "The fear of the Lord is the beginning of wisdom." Here, "fear" does not mean terror, but awe, reverence, and humility before God. Philosophically, it teaches that recognizing our human limits and the immensity of existence is the first step toward wisdom. Whether one sees it as spiritual grounding or simply an acknowledgment of reason's limits, the words resonated deeply with me. Thus, my study of the Shroud, what began as a scientific curiosity became something more. It bridged the gap between empirical observation and personal faith, leaving me with unanswered questions that science cannot resolve, while awakening a reverence I never expected to feel. Proceeding step by step my conclusions are rendered by areas covered.

The Provenance

After a long and difficult look at a mystery that has lasted hundreds if not thousands of years, it was time to review and contemplate the findings, I began with the provenance and chain of custody of the Shroud. In the category of chain of custody, the evidence is sparse at best. There is sparse documentation and unless we accept vague references to an image on a cloth we have very little to rely upon. Let's be careful to distinguish between true provenance and hypothetical reconstruction. The theories linking the Shroud to Edessa, Constantinople and Jerusalem are theories with some forensic evidence that includes pollen and dirt samples from the

Jerusalem area. The dirt samples do provide a link to the passion narrative and the pollen does link to the time frame in March- April in Jerusalem. Again, this is not definitive but closer to hypothetical reconstruction. Everything before the 1350s falls into the realm of tradition and hypothesis. Some crusader accounts mention cloth relics bearing the image of Christ after the sack of Constantinople. None can be securely identified as the Shroud. From 944–1204 Edessa/Constantinople: The "Image of Edessa" (Mandylion) is well-attested but some argue it was the Shroud folded to show only the face, but that is not universally accepted. Jerusalem (1st century): No documentary evidence connects the Turin Shroud directly to Jesus' burial or the earliest church. The verifiable chain begins in mid-14th-century France.

Before that, there is no secure record of this cloth. The first certain appearance happens when the Shroud is displayed in Lirey (Champagne) around 1355 by Geoffroy de Charny, a knight of France. The surviving pilgrim medallions from Lirey (with an image of the Shroud) confirms this exhibition. The local bishop (Henri de Poitiers) and later Pope Clement VII both reference it, showing it was known and controversial at the time. The House of Savoy (1453–1578) In 1453, Margaret de Charny (Geoffroy's granddaughter) gave the Shroud to Duke Louis of Savoy. It was then housed in Chambery, Savoy. The 1532 fire in the Sainte-Chapelle of Chambery damaged the cloth; it was repaired by Poor Clare nuns (the triangular burn marks visible today. In 1578, Duke Emmanuel Philibert transferred the Shroud to Turin, partly to make it easier for pilgrims (especially St. Charles Borromeo). Since then, it has remained in Turin Cathedral, under Savoy (and later Vatican) custody. This 1350s → present chain is secure, continuous, and undisputed.

Here we can conclude that the chain of custody and provenance of the Shroud is riddled with gaps making scientists and historians skeptical. The lack of definitive evidence of either the Shroud being from the 1st century or the actual burial cloth of Jesus cannot be proved from either the chain of custody with this chronological record or its provenance since its history of ownership cannot be properly determined.

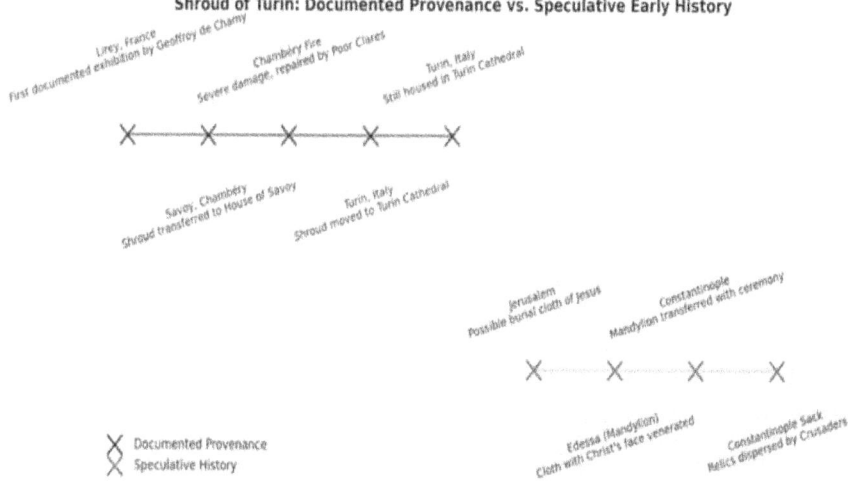

The Carbon 14 dating

In 1988, Carbon-14 dating was a robust scientific tool for dating recent archaeological and historical samples to a precision of ±100–200 years for material up to a few thousand years old, though it was always subject to inherent methodological assumptions, potential contamination, and the accuracy of calibration data. However, the carbon dating was not held to rigorous scientific standards The main issues I found are as follows:

The strip was taken from a single edge corner, which is not representative the entire cloth. Chemical analysis by Raymond Rogers (a STURP chemist) in 2005 revealed traces of cotton fibers, gum dye (madder root and aluminum oxide), and vanillin levels inconsistent with the main body, suggesting this area was a medieval repair via "invisible reweaving" by nuns after fire damage in 1532. If true, the dated material could be a patch from the 14th century, skewing results younger. Critics note that the protocol deviated from original plans for multiple sampling sites across the Shroud, reducing representativeness and violating standard practices for heterogeneous artifacts. Contamination is another key flaw. The Shroud has endured fires (notably in 1532, which scorched it and melted silver), smoke exposure, handling during displays, and centuries of storage, potentially introducing younger carbon. Bacterial biofilms or residues could add modern C-14, as bacteria incorporate atmospheric carbon postmortem; one study estimated this might require a layer doubling the sample weight to shift dates by 1,300 years, though pyrolysis-mass-spectrometry on Shroud fibers detected no such bioplastic polymers. However, experiments with carbon monoxide (from fires or candles) showed minimal impact under normal conditions, per Christopher Ramsey's 2008 follow-up tests.

The following flaw is, perhaps, the most severe in that the lack of peer review and release of the data for 29 year is inexcusable. The follow up statistical reanalysis have further eroded confidence and created the optic of hiding the flaws. Access to raw data (obtained via legal action against Oxford in 2017) revealed inter-laboratory heterogeneity and a monotonic spatial gradient in subsample ages, with dates increasing by about 36 years per centimeter across the strip, suggesting uneven contamination or cleaning pretreatments rather than a uniform medieval origin.

A 2019 study in Archaeometry concluded the data are inconsistent, invalidating the homogeneity assumption central to the 1988 conclusions. Earlier critiques, like a 2000 study by Russian scientist Dmitri Kouznetsov proposing carbon enrichment from heat, were debunked as irreproducible, but the raw data issues persist. As nuclear engineer Robert Rucker noted in recent analyses, these anomalies indicate the dating "does not match current accuracy requirements." Alternative dating methods have yielded older estimates. Giulio Fanti's 2013 infrared and spectroscopic tests on threads (purportedly from the 1988 samples) dated them to 300 BC–400 AD, though the chain of custody is disputed and the Shroud's custodian dismissed the findings. More robustly, Wide-Angle X-ray Scattering (WAXS) analysis in 2022 and 2024 by Liberato de Caro matched the Shroud's degradation to 1st-century linens from Masada (55–74 AD), avoiding C-14's contamination pitfalls as it's non-destructive and measures cellulose aging directly. These align with non-dating evidence favoring authenticity, such as pollen traces from the Jerusalem area, bloodstains consistent with crucifixion (Type AB with bilirubin from trauma), and pre-14th-century depictions like the 1192–1195 Pray Codex illustrating Shroud-like features. In a balanced assessment, the 1988 C-14 dating was groundbreaking for its time but compromised by protocol deviations, potential sampling bias, unresolved statistical inconsistencies, and the optics of impropriety, flaws substantial enough to question its conclusiveness. While no definitive proof exists that contamination or repairs altered the date by exactly 1,300 years (a high bar), the cumulative evidence from reanalysis and new techniques substantiates claims of unreliability. Skeptics rightly note that even a first-century date would not prove divine origin, as the Shroud contradicts Gospel accounts of multiple burial cloths (e.g., a separate face cloth in John 20:6–7). This argument, however, is countered with the Sudarium of Oviedo, which shares the same blood type and exhibits digitally matched staining with the Shroud.

To resolve the debate, new multi-site C-14 tests combined with WAXS on authenticated samples are warranted although, the Vatican has, understandably resisted further destructive sampling. As of 2025, the Shroud's age remains contested, but the 1988 results no longer stand as unassailable evidence of forgery. I would go further and argue that the combination of impropriety surrounding the British Museum's handling of the data, where records had to be released only through court order, together with the movement of senior officials previously discussed, completely negates the credibility of the Carbon 14 testing.

Some AI-driven claims (e.g., implying resurrection physics) are speculative and untestable, appearing in sensational videos rather than rigorous journals. AI has highlighted intriguing details supporting an ancient, radiation-formed image of a crucified man. The Catholic Church maintains no official stance, urging further study.

The Image:

The Shroud Image has two central questions: who is in the image and how was the image formed.

The first, question: who is it? The question is best approached by examining what is known of Roman Crucifixion, which was not commonly understood in medieval times. The proof that medieval people did not have in depth knowledge of crucifixions is readily apparent. This misunderstanding is still visible in most Christian households today. Look at a Crucifix hanging on the wall: crucifixes consistently show the nails placed in the palms of the hands. Every depiction is the same. Second, we look at the crown of thorns. Is the crown a full head cap or a wreath shaped around the head. Go back as far as you like and they are all the same. In reality, nails through the palms could not support a man's weight; Roman practice was through the wrists. Likewise, the crown of thorns is almost always shown as a circular wreath, whereas the Shroud suggests a cap-like structure covering the head. These inaccuracies, perpetuated across centuries, demonstrate that medieval artists lacked detailed knowledge of crucifixion. By contrast, the Shroud portrays precise details that align with the biblical accounts of Jesus' death. The correlation is too exact to be coincidental. How many men in history were crucified while mocked as "King"? Kings were almost never crucified. Crucifixion was reserved for slaves, rebels, and criminals of the lowest status. The detail in the Shroud clearly depicts one man and one man only, the historical Jesus of Nazareth. The biblical alignment is too exact to be coincidental to a different crucifixion. There is evidence the Romans often respected rank and crucifixion was a punishment for the lowest criminal. Rome occasionally showed leniency to high-ranking enemy commanders if they surrendered early or had political value.

For example, after the Battle of Actium (31 BC), some of Mark Antony's officers were spared or integrated into Octavian's regime, though this was rare and tied to political expediency rather than respect for their military rank. More often, high-ranking prisoners were used for propaganda, paraded in triumphs, and then executed or exiled, as with Syphax of Numidia after the Second Punic War (201 BC). Rome's respect for rank was heavily influenced by its perception of the enemy's culture. Soldiers from "civilized" societies like Greece or Egypt were sometimes treated with more consideration due to their perceived sophistication. Greek mercenaries or officers, for instance, might be ransomed or enslaved in roles like tutors, as their skills were valued. In contrast, soldiers from "barbarian" tribes like the Gaules or Britons were less likely to have their ranks acknowledged, often facing enslavement, slaughter or gladiator life unless they had strategic use (e.g. as auxiliaries). In conquered kingdoms, local military leaders could retain their positions if they swore allegiance to Rome. For example, in Mauretania, King Juba II's forces were reorganized under Roman command, and his soldiers served as auxiliaries. This preserved some semblance of rank but within a Roman framework, prioritizing loyalty over local hierarchy. The act of crucifixion was meant to make a public example of the victim in order to send a message of fear.

Pontius Pilot didn't think Jesus deserved such a punishment. The severity of the scourging was Pilots attempt to avoid crucifying Jesus. Pilot assumed the severely scourged man would satisfy the crowd. The argument that the Romans crucified so many men that there were others that fit that exact biblical description doesn't make sense. Further, if we look at the Shroud as a medieval art work then who where they trying to depict in their work? This again brings us back to Jesus of Nazareth. If the Shroud person is a model for a medieval artist, then, was he actually killed to create the pre and post mortem blood that exists on the Shroud. The more deeply we investigate the attributes of the Shroud the more preposterous the art work claims become. Science, however, insists upon extraordinary evidence and that evidence is slowly beginning to reveal the Shrouds secrets. We are just not there yet.

A personal journey into the mystery of the Shroud

What is the image and how was it formed?

This is, by far, the highest hurdle of this mystery. A team of top scientists after extensive study with the latest equipment could not answer that question. The only thing that they could add was to tell us what it is not. If we let that sink in for a minute. They couldn't tell us how the image was formed. If you believe the Shroud is 2000 years old or 700 years old the fact is modern science in the 20th and 21st century can't explain it or duplicate it. This piece of Linen is by far the most studied artifact in human history and that continues in 2025. The last attempt at recreating the Shroud was publicized in articles and the internet social media as having recreated the Shroud. We have covered the Bas-Relief model earlier which is the latest attempt to duplicate the Shroud. Bas relief does demonstrate a kind of negative image effect similar in conceptual terms to what is seen on the Shroud of Turin, but not the same phenomenon. The Shroud of Turin image is famously a photographic negative, meaning its light and dark tones are reversed compared to a normal positive image. This negative image effect can be visually striking and was an important clue to its photographic nature. Bas- Relief, on the other hand, is a form of low relief sculpture or an image made by combining a positive and a negative of the same image slightly out of register (offset) to create a three-dimensional effect. Bas relief, can produce an image with light and shadow contrasts resembling a negative or reversed tonal effect. In specific experiments related to the Shroud of Turin, researchers (STURP) demonstrated producing images by pressing wet cloth on a Bas-Relief sculpture and applying pigment to confirm that a bas-relief contact method could create images with shading and light patterns, somewhat like those on the Shroud, however no scorch marks or pigment exist on the Shroud. The Shroud image is noted for its three-dimensional character. The Shroud of Turin image is a photographic negative with encoded 3D information. The Shroud's negative photographic effect includes additional complexities beyond typical Bas- Relief. Therefore, Bas - Relief can demonstrate a negative image effect in the sense of tonal reversal and some three-dimensional shading, but the Shroud's negative image has a distinct photographic and mysterious encoding quality that goes beyond simple Bas- Relief.

When it comes to the wound details, the Bas-Relief method, especially when heated or scorched, falls short. Experiments show that heating a Bas-Relief to transfer an image tends to produce "hot spots," burning marks, or blurred discoloration rather than the subtle gradations and clear anatomical details seen in the Shroud's wounds. No such marks appear on the Shroud. Moreover, the wound bloodstains on the Shroud do not exhibit signs of thermal alteration, which would be expected if a hot Bas- Relief had been used.

Further the Shroud's image is on the blood stain which indicates the blood came first. Adding blood to a Bas-Relief will have the blood over the image. Cicero Moraes' low-relief model does not specifically address or claim to reproduce the bloodstain patterns on the Shroud of Turin. His study focused on how the cloth draped over a low-relief sculpture versus a real human body could explain the main body image on the Shroud, showing that the low-relief imprint is more consistent with the Shroud's anatomical patterns and less distorted than fabric draping over a true 3D body. However, Moraes' work did not investigate or replicate the bloodstains, which are a separate complex aspect of the Shroud's image. Some scholars have pointed out that the physical and chemical complexities of the bloodstains—such as flow patterns and composition—cannot be accounted for by the simple low-relief contact model.

Over years of studying various projects, I have consistently encountered resistance and reluctance to change. In banking system design, users often resisted new platforms due to fear of the unknown or attachment to familiar systems. Similarly, my exploration of the Shroud of Turin revealed multifaceted resistance rooted in financial, reputational, and institutional concerns. The following examines the sources of resistance to scientific inquiry into the Shroud, the possible motives behind maintaining ambiguity, and my personal reflections on how this investigation reshaped my perspective. Maybe resistance is fear from moving away from something that is known and comfortable. I found a different resistance in looking at the Billy the Kid legend. This resistance was a push back for financial and reputational risk associated with a change in the status quo. The Shroud has its own resistance, religious and institutional tensions.

The Shroud of Turin Research Project (STURP), which conducted extensive scientific analysis in 1978, faced subtle but significant opposition for instance, the allegation of strong Catholic affiliation of many STURP members led to suspicions and critiques about potential bias. Conflicts arose even within the team, as some members like John Heller and McCrone had personal and scientific disagreements on interpreting the evidence. While there was no organized external group openly opposing the physical examination during the actual 1978 testing, there were behind-the-scenes concerns and political pressures, including from some Vatican authorities and conservative elements worried about the implications of the findings.

Upon examination of the accusation of strong catholic affiliation among the STURP team I found the following: Of the "STURP ten", the leaders and core scientists of the Shroud of Turin Research Project, four were Catholic.

Religious Breakdown of the STURP Team

- According to Dr. John Heller, one of the key STURP scientists, the breakdown was "six agnostics, two Mormons, three Jews, four Catholics and all the rest Protestants." While the overall project involved about thirty to forty scientists, this distribution referred specifically to the central leadership and most active members.

- Other sources confirm that John Jackson (team leader) and Eric Jumper, two of the project's prime movers, were indeed Catholics.

The composition of the team was intentionally diverse, chosen for scientific skills rather than religious belief. Catholics held important leadership roles, but there was no religious litmus test for participation. Many STURP members, regardless of faith, had little previous exposure to the Shroud, and most formed their opinions based on the scientific process and were agnostic.

Unlike the period of the STURP examination where ownership of the Shroud was with the royal family of Italy. The carbon dating took place under the ownership of the Pope and controlled by the Vatican. The Shroud was owned by the Holy See, so any testing required Vatican approval. Cardinal Anastasio Ballestrero, Archbishop of Turin, authorized the sampling and oversaw logistics. The Vatican agreed to the testing but restricted the sample to a single site (the corner near the edge, cut from one piece). Originally, a broader range of samples was proposed, including threads from different areas of the cloth by the STURP team.

This brings up suspicion of manipulation. The first thought that comes to mind is why would the Vatican want to manipulate the results of the validation of what is possibly the most important relic of their faith? The Vatican's motive would not necessarily be to manipulate the results in one direction (authentic vs fake), but rather to control the narrative. By restricting the tests and ensuring ambiguity, the Church preserves the Shroud's spiritual power without risking a definitive scientific verdict. If the Shroud is authentic there are possible motives to delay or deflect definitive proof. The Vatican has historically been cautious about scientific "proof" of relics and the Shroud has never been declared a "dogma", only an object of veneration that "represents" Christ. If it were proven authentic, it could elevate the Shroud into a doctrinal battlefield, potentially forcing the Church into defending something that might later be contradicted by new evidence. By permitting tests but restricting samples, the Vatican may have been seeking a "plausible uncertainty", allowing scientific study but preventing closure.

If the Shroud is not authentic the possible motive is likely to protect devotion. The Church is not dependent on the Shroud, but it is a major focus of pilgrimage, devotion, and revenue. A firm conclusion that it's a medieval fake could harm popular devotion and embarrass the Church. By controlling access and protocol, the Vatican could reduce the chance of a definitive "fake" verdict by limiting the sample size, enabling criticism while ensuring the mystery (and devotion) remains alive. These are all speculative scenarios defining possible states of nature. The Vatican has centuries of precedent in keeping relics in the realm of faith rather than forensic science. Another possible explanation has nothing to do with the findings at all. The Vatican had come into possession of the Shroud within five years of the testing and there was no desire to mutilate what may be the single most important relic in Church history. The process of Carbon 14 dating destroys the samples. Their priority may not have been to prove or disprove authenticity but to preserve the status quo, to keep the Shroud as an object of faith without being locked into a scientific conclusion. Individuals and groups outside of the Vatican had motives to see the radiocarbon dating not resolve the question, whether to protect faith, preserve reputation, or maintain mystery. But the evidence suggests this wasn't sabotage in a conspiratorial sense; it was more a matter of pressures and interests converging to favor ambiguity rather than definitive closure.

Groups like the Shroud of Turin Research Project (STURP), made up of scientists and enthusiasts who had studied the Shroud since 1978, were largely convinced the cloth was ancient. They opposed radiocarbon dating from a single corner sample, arguing it could be contaminated, rewoven, or unrepresentative. Many feared a "bad protocol" would damage the credibility of the Shroud, so some openly criticized or resisted the test design even before results were published. Their interest was not in sabotaging science, but in preventing a flawed, oversimplified verdict that could mislead the public. Financial interests can also not be ignored. The Shroud has been central to Turin's identity, pilgrimages, and prestige for centuries. A firm "medieval fake" result could have meant a loss of religious tourism and prestige. While they couldn't stop the test (the Vatican was the owner), they had an incentive to favor uncertainty over closure. Some secular researchers worried about the repercussions if the Shroud was proven authentic. Such a result would have been explosive impact on the worlds religious communities, potentially used as scientific proof of Christ's resurrection. The convergence of these pressures, religious, financial, and cultural, again suggests a preference for ambiguity over clarity.

The Vatican, Turin's stakeholders, and the media all benefit from an unresolved mystery. The Church preserves the Shroud's spiritual power, scientists maintain research relevance, Turin sustains tourism, and the media capitalizes on intrigue. These dynamic echoes historical patterns, where relics remain objects of faith rather than forensic certainty.

Most problematic to me, is the media and the public narrative. The media have, in the 21st century, become very controversial. The reporting of facts has become secondary to sensationalism and the need to generate ratings in order to generate revenue. The Shroud has always been surrounded by mystery. A definitive "yes" or "no" could kill the drama. Journalists, authors, and even some church figures may have preferred that testing remain inconclusive, because ambiguity sustains public fascination and keeps the Shroud in headlines. However, upon receiving a no verdict, headlines all over the world printed the sensational headline of HOAX.

None of this appears to be new, going all the way back to Bishop Pierre d'Arcis of Troy claiming a supposed artist's confession of forgery. This artist supposedly created this one-of-a-kind work and never did anything again. Clearly agendas have run rampant for centuries and apparently still exist. What I find unusual is the willingness to submit nonsense as the solution to the mystery. Not as unusual is the media's willingness to broadcast these "solutions" as credible. Fortunately, science itself cannot be held in check. New technologies are presenting themselves as formidable opponents of status quo. As I have described, a mystery should not stay a mystery because of an agenda. I believe this mystery may prove to be the most powerful of them all.

At first, I approached the Shroud merely as a mystery to solve. But soon, it evoked an unexpected blend of fear and introspection. In seeking to understand its significance, I read the Bible from cover to cover for the first time. This revealed a cohesive narrative of forgiveness and redemption, spanning from the Old Testament's stories of Israel's restoration to the New Testament's focus on Christ's resurrection. I discovered a deeper flow within these Stories, messages embedded in proverbs, parables, and the prophets that I had never before recognized or connected. Throughout both Testaments, a consistent theme emerged: forgiveness and redemption from a merciful God. Although the Israelites often strayed and faced divine punishment, God's forgiveness was always present, a pattern prompting profound personal reflection. What began as a project to unravel a mystery transformed into an unexpected journey of self-reflection. Compelled, surprisingly, I felt driven to share my Shroud project with anyone willing to listen, perhaps in search of help unlocking its meaning. Most people I spoke to regarded the Shroud as proof of the Resurrection. Gradually, I reconsidered this perspective: perhaps resurrection is one message among several. The Shroud's testimony to redemption is neither contradicted nor disproven by science; in many ways, it is subtly affirmed. Scientific analysis may not yield courtroom-style proof, but it uncovers an ever-deepening recognition.

The Shroud of Turin occupies a unique crossroads between faith and science. Christians have venerated it for centuries as the burial cloth of Jesus Christ, a silent witness to both his passion and resurrection, while skeptics dismiss it as legend or medieval curiosity. Yet as science advanced, the mystery only deepened. Like exposing layers, the Shroud reveals its secrets slowly, beckoning continued inquiry. It seems to testify to a transformative event that defies ordinary explanation. If the Shroud's message unfolds hand-in-hand with technological progress, perhaps it was designed to reveal its full meaning only to future generations. In the first century, the themes of passion and resurrection were not obvious. When Secondo Pia first photographed the Shroud in 1898, the haunting negative image unveiled striking details invisible to the naked eye. What previously appeared as a faint imprint became a vivid, three-dimensional portrait of a crucified man, an effect impossible for any medieval artist to have conceived or created. Thereafter, the Shroud began to speak not only as an icon of devotion but as an enigma beyond early scientific explanation.

The image itself remains the greatest puzzle: studies confirm it is neither painted, dyed, nor etched, lying only on the outermost fibrils of the linen, thinner than a human hair, with no underlying pigment. Researchers have hypothesized bursts of energy, ultraviolet radiation, or phenomena beyond current physics. Its creation seems beyond ordinary artistic methods, perhaps even beyond natural laws as we understand them. At this convergence of faith and science, faith proclaims the resurrection a moment where death was overcome, while science limited by its tools neither confirms nor denies the resurrection but acknowledges an unexplained phenomenon. Some believers find, in this convergence, a gradual unveiling of a truth larger than science itself. The Shroud's enduring message is that suffering and death are real, but they are not the final word. In its mystery, the cloth whispers of transformation: redemption and resurrection are not myths but profound realities, which science in its slow exploration is beginning to acknowledge.

The Shroud's message reflects the heart of Easter, a journey from darkness to light, from death to life. As scientific inquiry evolves, the Shroud's testimony grows clearer, echoing Christianity's central promise, not merely that resurrection is possible but that it has occurred. Early on, I dismissed claims that the Shroud "proved the resurrection," viewing the evidence as incomplete and the arguments as blending faith with fact. Yet the deeper I delved, the more evidence seemed to accumulate with each scientific discovery. It was only in 1978 that science definitively established that the Shroud is not a painting. For these reasons, I can no longer dismiss its testimony to the resurrection, despite the absence of absolute scientific proof. I realized that while I sought to avoid letting faith bias my interpretation, I must equally guard against bias borne of opposition to faith. Throughout the Old Testament, the concept of "being raised up" symbolizes God's work in reviving or restoring his people, both individually and collectively. Passages like Hosea 6:2 ("After two days he will revive us; on the third day he will raise us up, that we may live before him") and Lamentations 5:21

("Restore us to yourself, O Lord, that we may be restored!") emphasize themes of national and spiritual renewal. God calls his people to rise after adversity, whether from destruction or exile, as modeled in the narratives of the Exodus and the return from Babylon. Symbolic acts such as rising incense and ascending offerings reinforce this vertical connection between humanity and the divine. God "raises up" individuals (e.g. judges in Judges 2:16) and exalts the downtrodden (the "horn" lifted, a metaphor for restored honor in Psalm 92:10 and 1 Samuel 2:1). Raised hands in prayer (Psalm 28:2; 134:2) express visible gestures of surrender and invocation.

The New Testament magnifies these themes, placing Christ's resurrection at center stage, Jesus is "raised" from the dead, promising new life to believers. He teaches about exalting the humble and spiritual rebirth, emphasizing a pattern of being lifted by God. The epistles build on this assurance, affirming that those "in Christ" are "raised with him" (Ephesians 2:6; Colossians 3:1), not only for future resurrection but for present transformation and growth. Calls to "lift up" hands, voices, and hearts saturate Scripture, symbolizing surrender, adoration, and dependence. The ultimate climax is Jesus's literal "resurrection, raised from the dead" (Matthew 28:6; 1 Corinthians 15:52), the foundation of Christian faith.

My research led to personal transformation. Immersing myself in scholarship, I turned to Scripture for insight into the Shroud's meaning and found a unifying narrative of forgiveness and redemption flowing from Proverbs and the prophets, stories I had never previously linked. Redemption through sacrifice emerges as a clear, recurrent theme threading through both Testaments. In the Old

Testament, blood sacrifices secure atonement (Leviticus 17:11), and messianic prophecies, especially Isaiah 53, speak of one "pierced for our transgressions." The Passover lamb (Exodus 12) becomes a pattern for the sacrificial Messiah. Daniel 9:24-27 foretells the Messiah would be "cut off, but not for himself," confirming his death secures redemption and ends the need for animal sacrifices. The New Testament presents Jesus as fulfilling these prophecies. He speaks of giving his life "as a ransom for many" (Mark 10:45) and frames his death as a sacrifice at the Last Supper ("This is my blood... poured out for many for the remission of sins," Matthew 26:28). The epistles interpret his death as the once-for-all act of salvation (Romans 5:8; Hebrews 9:12). This seamless flow between Testaments, embodied in redemption through blood, marks the heart of Christian tradition. Whether authentic or not, the Shroud transmits this message: love's cost, death's reality, and the promise of new life.

The suffering depicted on the Shroud struck me with vivid realism: wounds consistent with scourging, crucifixion, and the crown of thorns. These are not abstract marks; they reveal the extremes of human suffering and injustice. Redemption, in Christian understanding, begins here. The lifeless body, with its wounds, testifies to the undeniable cost of love. The image's faint, almost luminous quality hints at a moment of transformation, a visual whisper of resurrection. The message of redemption is accessible even to skeptics. The Shroud's bloodstains have been verified as authentic human blood, type AB, with trauma indicators consistent with crucifixion. Even those who argue for a medieval origin acknowledge how accurately the wounds align with Roman execution customs. In an age fixated on empirical proof, the Shroud invites appreciation of sacrificial suffering, independently of miraculous claims. For modern societies grappling with violence, injustice, and the yearning for redemption, whether in therapy, justice systems, or popular culture's narratives, the Shroud's message is timely. Its forensic detail grounds atonement in something immediate and tangible, confronting us with the brutal cost and reality of love.

For believers and skeptics alike, redemption emerges as the Shroud's primary message, a message rooted in suffering, verified in blood, and echoed in Gospel accounts (Mark 15:15-39; Isaiah 53:5; Hebrews 9:22). This message requires no supernatural leap; it presents a visible, forensic record of ultimate sacrifice. The narrative flow is both chronological and theological: redemption, demonstrated in Christ's death and mirrored in the Shroud, must precede the resurrection. The New Testament intensifies this theme, centering on Christ's resurrection, believers are "raised" with him, promised a new life. Jesus teaches about lifting up the humble and spiritual rebirth, patterns of elevation by God. The epistles affirm that those "in Christ" experience present moral transformation and future resurrection, shaping lives oriented toward "things above." Christ's resurrection, a literal raising from death, is the foundation of Christian faith and promise of eternal life (Matthew 28:6; 1 Corinthians 15:52). His own language of "being lifted up" (John 12:32-33) draws on Old Testament imagery, like Moses lifting the serpent (Numbers 21:4-9), symbolizing the crucifixion as a means of spiritual salvation (John 3:14).

As I dug deeper into the Shroud, I sensed shifts in my perception. After exploring several books and Scripture, the messages of the Shroud felt different, flowing beyond the obvious with hidden layers in Proverbs, parables, and prophecy. This stirred reflection on my own life. What began as a mystery unveiled a call to share my findings, which was unusual for me, suggesting an unconscious search for insight. The overarching theme pointed clearly to the Messiah's sacrifice for redemption, spanning both Testaments. Sacrificial blood, central to atonement in Leviticus 17:11, and messianic prophecies like Isaiah 53 anticipate one who bears others' sins. The Passover lamb prefigures the Messiah's substitute sacrifice. Daniel's prophecy of the "cut off" Messiah foretells the final redemptive act ending animal sacrifices. The New Testament sees Jesus fulfilling these prophecies, giving his life "as a ransom for many" (Mark 10:45) and instituting the new covenant in his blood (Matthew 26:28). Apostolic writings interpret Jesus' death as the ultimate sacrifice securing eternal redemption (Romans 5:8; Hebrews 9:12). Early preaching links Psalms and Isaiah to Jesus' suffering and resurrection, establishing redemptive necessity. This continuity between Testaments centers on redemption by blood, a foundational Christian doctrine. The Shroud, authentic or not, communicates this profound message.

My investigation revealed the Shroud's suffering in striking detail: scourging, crucifixion wounds, a crown of thorns. These embody the extremity of human pain and injustice. Redemption, from a Christian view, starts in this shared human brokenness. The lifeless body affirms death's reality but also the passage through which redemption emerges. The image's faint glow suggests resurrection, a visual echo of overcoming death. The Shroud's message transcends belief; it speaks of an innocent suffering for others, love through sacrifice, and transformation beyond death.

Scientific debate surrounds the image's creation, with hypotheses including bursts of energy or radiation. Yet redemption remains the more immediate message today. In an age defined by skepticism, empirical inquiry, and a search for meaning amid suffering, redemption resonates deeply. I argue that redemption is the Shroud's "first part" message, grounded in forensic detail, historical resonance, and cultural relevance. These align precisely with Gospel accounts of Jesus' passion (Mark 15:15-39), emphasizing atoning suffering central to Christian theology. Christ's blood redeems humanity (Isaiah 53:5; Hebrews 9:22), and the bloodstains on the Shroud have been verified as real human blood, type AB, with male DNA and trauma indicators. Even skeptics acknowledge the anatomical accuracy aligned with first-century executions. In a world grappling with violence, injustice, and personal redemption, restorative justice, and cultural narratives. The Shroud's forensic suffering invites reflection without requiring belief in miracles. It grounds atonement in visceral experience. Redemption flows naturally from the Shroud's undisputed features: the body's posture in death, blood flow consistent with crucifixion, and absence of decomposition suggesting brief cloth contact.

Theologically, redemption precedes resurrection, Good Friday before Easter Sunday. For many today, often secular or disillusioned, the Shroud's redemption message is an entry point, prompting "What does this suffering mean?" before "How was this image made?" This resembles contemporary faith encounters, through personal redemption stories rather than proofs of the divine. In a world challenged by crises, the Shroud's depiction of redemptive suffering is a symbol of hope through endurance. Theological interpreters call it a "silent witness" to Christ's atoning work, emphasizing redemption as the primary message for a doubting world. Unlike resurrection, which can seem abstract or escapist, redemption addresses universal human experiences: guilt, forgiveness, and transformation. The Shroud's serene facial expression amid brutality suggests willing sacrifice, inviting viewers to see their own struggles as redeemable. Critics may dismiss the Shroud as a medieval forgery, but its message of redemption endures as a cultural artifact inspiring art, literature, and ethics. For believers and skeptics alike, it first confronts the cost of love and justice, paving the way for the deeper mystery of resurrection as evidence accumulates.

The concept of cost resonated deeply with me. People in the 1st century followed Jesus, witnessed his miracles of healing and raising the dead, yet his ultimate mission, requiring a price, seemed overshadowed. Even his apostles asked where he was going and why they could not follow. These were people who saw, heard, and touched him, yet did not fully grasp what was to come. The Shroud's image serves as a mirror of the Gospel, symbolizing Christ's suffering and sacrificial death for humanity's sins. Many interpret this visual "witness" as a tangible sign of redemption, through Jesus' suffering and crucifixion, humanity is offered forgiveness and reconciliation with God. In an era of technological progress, moral questioning, and spiritual skepticism, this silent testimony transcends words.

The Shroud's second message, resurrection, remains under scientific investigation. Some interpret the image as evidence of an intense burst of radiation at resurrection, but scientific consensus remains unresolved. New studies explore whether vacuum ultraviolet radiation caused the Shroud's unique features, including its negative image and fiber discoloration. Remarkable as these findings are, science has neither confirmed nor refuted resurrection's reality. I believe advances in artificial intelligence and quantum computing will soon provide proof of the Shroud's resurrection message.

Chapter 11: The Shroud as a Time Capsule

What, then, is the Shroud of Turin? In my search, I was forced to reinterpret the very nature of its message Taken together, these dual messages make the Shroud not just a relic but a purposeful time capsule: it presents, first, a call to redemption in the modern era and, second, an unresolved scientific enigma that points toward the resurrection, awaiting future discovery. The unresolved scientific nature of the resurrection serves as both a challenge and an invitation to future generations to confront the central mystery of Christianity, not only in faith but also through the tools of science. My opinion is the Shroud was not created to be meaningful to its first-century witnesses, who lacked the knowledge and technology to decipher its secrets. Instead, it was crafted for our time. As the modern era has advanced, equipped with digital imaging, particle physics, and artificial intelligence, new details of the Shroud's messages have slowly emerged. We now see what ancient eyes could not: anatomical impossibilities for a medieval forger, Middle Eastern pollen and fibers, x-ray–like qualities, and a haunting echo of the suffering described in Scripture. The Shroud's history is tangled, its trail marked by gaps and mysteries, yet within those gaps emerges a pattern. Pollen unique to ancient Jerusalem, matching bloodstains with the Sudarium of Oviedo, and enduring mysteries of its weave and three-dimensional image formation all forge circumstantial, yet powerful, links to antiquity. Even the famous radiocarbon dating, once hailed as definitive, now stands as flawed. New scientific advances, like Wide-Angle X-ray Scattering (WAXS), have revitalized debate, suggesting the linen is roughly 2,000 years old. First and foremost, the Shroud documents, in the most literal, physical detail, the cost of redemption. It is covered in the wounds of crucifixion, precisely as described in the Gospel narratives. Its bloodstains, verified as real, are the cost paid for humanity's liberation from sin. This message is timeless, but its forensic precision is designed for an age steeped in skepticism, reason, and empirical proof, the very age in which we live. Mainstream consensus remains elusive, but skepticism about the medieval dating now rivals the skepticism once reserved for authenticity. The age of the Shroud remains an open question.

Science reaches Its limits

AI has begun identifying subtle details beyond human observational capacity, suggesting that deeper insights may emerge as technology advances. AI is not a Catholic or even a Christian for that matter. However, it has found that the Shroud is a precise, negative, anatomically and mathematically accurate "photograph" of a crucified man, bearing all the signs of roman execution, with wounds that match both Gospel accounts and medical analysis. The level of information encoded in the linen material is far beyond what a medieval artist or modern science ability to encode on a linen material. This also opens the subject of if linen can hold encoded information, then maybe other forms of matter also have that capability. Scientific efforts to replicate the image, even with AI and laser technology, have only affirmed its uniqueness. The image resides on the outermost fibers, is three-dimensional, and encodes details invisible to the medieval world. Attempts to explain the origin of the image have failed. Artistic techniques, chemical vapors, Bas-Relief models, all fall short. The most persuasive scientific theory points to a burst of ultraviolet radiation: a flash so sudden, so powerful, and yet so finely tuned that technology today can only barely mimic it, and even then, at energy levels beyond the realms of possibility in our era. Science, for all its advances, stands humbled before this ancient witness.

The second message is not yet fully unwrapped. Science, despite its advances, has not explained the image's formation. In this, the Shroud extends a challenge: it points to a resurrection, not yet confirmed by science, but persistently witnessed by the artifact itself. AI and quantum computing may, one day, unlock this riddle. Until then, the Shroud keeps its second message partially veiled, beckoning us toward truths at the very limits of understanding.

Unlike relics that demand only veneration, the Shroud invites encounter, reflection, even skepticism. It does not command belief, but provokes it. Like the wound Christ offered to Thomas, it is evidence meant for those who must "see to believe", a call tailored for the doubting spirit of our own era. Far from a relic for medieval pilgrims, the Shroud of Turin is the world's oldest and most sophisticated time capsule, a message crafted to outlast empires and skepticism, intended to be opened just as the 21st century's scientific achievements reach the doorstep of the extraordinary. As science presses ever closer to the truth, the Shroud's meaning deepens: It is a record of the immense price paid for love and forgiveness. It is the cipher for resurrection, its solution still to come and it is a silent challenge to a generation obsessed with proof: an enduring witness, preserved for when the world was finally ready to see.

The radiation theory is based on a process of elimination; other proposed causes such as chemical reactions, vapors, heat, paint, or scorching have been ruled out because the image only resides on the uppermost fibers of the cloth without penetrating deeper or scorching it. Radiation burst could have created a perfect, anatomically detailed, 3D negative image on both the front and back of the cloth, even coloring fibers in regions not touching the body.

This level of radiation and the way it interacted with the linen fibers explain many of the image's unique characteristics, including its presence only on surface fibers and its similarity to an X-ray effect revealing details beneath the skin. Experiments with lasers and UV photons have shown the plausibility of such light-based mechanisms in recreating effects similar to the Shroud's image. However, the exact cause of this radiation burst remains unexplained by any known natural human or physical process.

However, I became convinced of one thing: whatever the Shroud's message is, it was not meant for first-century Christians. Perhaps, it's a message from Jesus himself for a scientific, skeptical age. It is both a proof of redemption and a time-sealed challenge about resurrection, meant to provoke awe, humility, and ultimately faith. As humanity itself reaches for answers that time has kept just beyond our grasp. The Shroud presents itself as a "receipt" for that transaction, the itemized ledger, of suffering required for redemption, a physical testament to the price paid for reconciliation between God and humanity. What, other than the resurrection, was Jesus' mission? Well Jesus' mission wasn't the resurrection at all it was the redemption of mankind. Jesus demonstrated raising people from the dead throughout scripture with the story of Lazarus being the most prominent. While the resurrection remains as a key belief and a core of the Christian faith Jesus didn't come to us just to demonstrate he could defeat death.

Redemption, at its heart, refers to Christ's saving work through his suffering and death on the Cross, by which humanity is freed from sin and reconciled with God. Through his death, Christ bore the penalty of our sin, satisfying divine justice and opening the way to forgiveness. As the Church teaches: "By his death, Christ liberates us from sin". Yet redemption cannot be understood in terms of the Cross alone. Liberation from sin is not the same as new life. Without the Resurrection, the Cross remains incomplete. The Resurrection is the climactic event of salvation history, the victory over death and the crowning fulfillment of Christ's redemptive mission.

In this light, the Shroud appears to bear witness to both Redemption and Resurrection. Its silent testimony functions like an itemized ledger, displaying in graphic detail the immeasurable cost of our salvation. The Shroud attests to the price Christ paid on our behalf. It does not speak in parables or symbols alone but confronts us with tangible evidence that demands reflection, challenges modern skepticism, and deepens the wisdom yet to unfold. While 21st-century science has neither proven nor disproven that the Shroud was formed by a supernatural event, technological advances continue to bring us closer to solving that mystery. Yet one message of the Shroud is already undeniable: with haunting precision, it reveals the immense pain and suffering endured for our redemption.

As technology evolves, I believe an even greater revelation will one day emerge. This final message will not arrive through human ingenuity alone, but through an intelligence far beyond even the brightest scientific minds. It is the same truth that the first disciples encountered in the most direct and convincing way possible. They did not need the Shroud because they saw the risen Christ with their own eyes. That encounter so transformed them that they devoted the rest of their lives, and ultimately surrendered those lives, to proclaiming his resurrection.

Man has prided himself as the superior intellect of the planet and scientists have positioned themselves as the keepers of the truth. The same scientists, when in the past, claimed the Earth flat and if man was meant to fly, he would have wings. Today things are a bit different, scientists claim that the universe resulted from a "Big Bang". That was, of course, prior to the James Webb telescope poking holes in that theory. How about when the Hubble telescope was launched and scientists, for the first time, had a much clearer view of the universe and what did they see? They saw this at the Center of the Whirlpool Galaxy (M51)

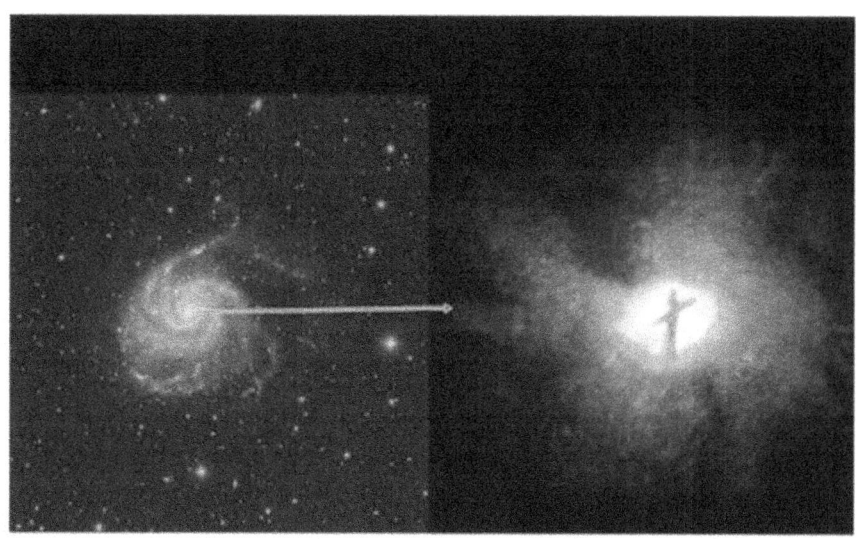

Does this look familiar?

They named it the Hubble cross at the core of the Whirlpool Galaxy (M51), which is a separate spiral galaxy located about 20 to 25

million light-years away from Earth. The size of the Hubble cross structure in the core of the Whirlpool Galaxy (M51) is approximately 1100 light-years across. Science tells us to forget what it looks like; this is what it is. Until new facts surface and prove them wrong again. I don't mean to be overly critical of our scientific disciplines. I just want to point out that we are living in a rapidly changing environment that is about to undergo massive transformation with the advent of AI Quantum computing. In my opinion, the ultimate proof of the Resurrection message of the Shroud is forthcoming. For me, the project that started as an investigation of a mystery has ended in a profound peace that I cannot explain.

In the time of the apostles, the Shroud carried little meaning. Standing in the presence of the risen Lord, a tangible cloth could add nothing to what they already knew. But its significance is preserved for future generations, generations like ours, who have not seen him in the flesh and must wrestle with belief through signs, testimony, and faith. Scripture has carried forward the living Word, bearing the message across centuries. But the Shroud endures as something different; not just a symbol, but a silent witness. It is as if Christ left us not only His Word, but also His Receipt. A full itemized receipt of the price he paid for the salvation of mankind and an enduring proof of payment in full.

Bibliography

Primary Sources

Ballestrero, Anastasio. La Sindone: Un Mistero Che Interroga la Scienza e la Fede. Torino: Edizioni Paoline, 1989.

De Charny, Geoffroy II. Attestation Letters of 1389–1390 Regarding the Shroud of Turin. Transcriptions and translations in Shroud archival collections.

Hall, Edward. Statements Regarding the Oxford Radiocarbon Dating Laboratory and the Endowment of the Edward Hall Chair of Archaeological Science. Oxford University Archives, 1989.

Shroud of Turin Research Project (STURP). Final Report and Recommendations on Sampling Protocols for Radiocarbon Dating the Turin Shroud. 1986.

"STURP's Published Papers." Shroud.com. Accessed 2025. https://www.shroud.com/78papers.htm.

Tite, Michael J. "The Shroud of Turin: Radiocarbon Dating Results." British Museum Press Release, 1988.

"Charny Manuscripts and the Book of Geoffroi de Charny." Cambridge: Cambridge University Press, 2021.

"Why Did Geoffroy de Charny Change His Mind?" Shroud.com. Accessed 2025.

Secondary Sources (Scholarly / Forensic Works)

Adler, A. D. "Blood Chemistry Studies on the Turin Shroud." Shroud Spectrum International, no. 28–29 (1988): 18–27.

Baima Bollone, P. "New Insights on Blood Evidence from the Turin Shroud Consistent with Jesus Christ's Tortures." Archives of Hematology Case Reports and Reviews 9, no. 1 (2024). https://www.clinsurggroup.us/articles/AHCRR-9-144.php.

Beard, Mary, John North, and Simon Price. Religions of Rome: Volume 1, A History. Cambridge: Cambridge University Press, 1998.

Benford, M., and Joe Marino, eds. Shroud Spectrum International. Various issues. Shroud.com.

Bucklin, R. "Some Observations on the Medical Aspects of the Shroud of Turin." Marquette University e-Publications. Accessed 2025. https://epublications.marquette.edu/cgi/viewcontent.cgi?article=3638&context=lnq.

Casabianca, Tristan. "Systematic Evaluation of Recent Research on the Shroud of Turin." Phil Archive, 2024. https://philarchive.org/archive/CASSEO-2.

Casabianca, Tristan, et al. "Radiocarbon Dating of the Turin Shroud: New Evidence from Raw Data." Archaeometry 61, no. 5 (2019): 1223–31.

Cazelles, Henry. The Shroud of Lirey: Historical Investigations. In various Shroud research anthologies.

Damon, P. E., et al. "Radiocarbon Dating of the Shroud of Turin." Nature 337, no. 6208 (1989): 611–15.

Di Costanzo, Jacques. Le Suaire de Turin: L'empreinte d'un Crucifié. Marseille: Editions Tacussel, 1991.

Di Lazzaro, P., D. Murra, and A. Santoni. "Some Experiments and Remarks Regarding the Possible Formation of Blood Stains on the Turin Shroud: Stains Attributed to the Crown of Thorns, the Lance Wound and the Belt of Abuse." International Journal of Legal Medicine, 2023.

"Some Experiments and Remarks Regarding the Possible Formation of Blood Stains on the Turin Shroud: Stains Attributed to the Nailing of the Hands." Forensic Science International: Reports, 2024.

Faccini, B. "Scourge Bloodstains on the Turin Shroud: An Evidence for Different Instruments Used." Shroud.com. Accessed 2025.

Fanti, G. "How Was the Turin Shroud Man Crucified?" Injury 46, no. 6 (2014): 1038–48.

Fanti, G., and P. Malfi. "The Shroud of Turin: An Overview of the Archaeological Scientific Research and Results." Heritage 5, no. 1 (2025): 94–125.

Garza-Valdés, Leoncio A. The DNA of God? New York: Doubleday, 1999.

Garnsey, Peter. Social Status and Legal Privilege in the Roman Empire. Oxford: Clarendon Press, 1970.

Gibbon, Edward. The History of the Decline and Fall of the Roman Empire. Edited by David Womersley. London: Penguin Classics, 1994.

Gilbert, Maurice. The Crucifixion Image: The Shroud of Turin. London: Scala Books, 1991.

Heller, John H. Report on the Shroud of Turin. Boston: Houghton Mifflin, 1983.

Hengel, Martin. Crucifixion in the Ancient World and the Folly of the Message of the Cross. Philadelphia: Fortress Press, 1977.

Jackson, John P., and Eric Jumper. The Shroud of Turin: An Adventure of Discovery. Colorado Springs: Shroud Center of Colorado, 1990.

La Greca, F., and L. De Caro. "The Shroud of Turin Blood Marks as a Case Example: Compatibility of the Calcified or Bio-Plastic Coating Hypothesis with the Presence of Cellulose between the Fibers." Forensic Science International: Reports 11 (2025).

Lavoie, DD. Gilbert. "The Shroud of Jesus" Sophia Institute Press 2023

Marinelli, Fabrizio. "The Lirey Controversy: Authenticity and Ownership of the Shroud of Turin." Journal of Medieval Religious Studies 29, no. 2 (2010).

Marino, Joseph G. "1988 C-14 Dating of the Shroud of Turin a Stunning Expose" 2020

Mattingly, David J. "Bacterial Contamination Hypothesis and the Shroud of Turin." Shroud Spectrum International, no. 42 (1993).

McCrone, Walter. Judgment Day for the Turin Shroud. Chicago: Microscope Publications, 1996.

Meacham, William. The Authentication of the Turin Shroud. Various articles and summaries. Shroud.com.

Moraes, Cicero. Faces of the Shroud: A Digital Reconstruction. São Paulo: Arc-Team Press, 2022.

Nickell, Joe. Inquest on the Shroud of Turin. 2nd ed. Amherst, NY: Prometheus Books, 1992.

Stevenson, Kenneth E., and Gary R. Habermas. "The Shroud of Turin: An Introduction." In Christian Origins and the Rule of Faith, 1–25. Grand Rapids, MI: Baker Academic, 2003.

Walsh, John Evangelist. The Shroud: 2000 Years of History. New York: Random House, 1963.

Wilson, Ian. The Shroud of Turin: The Burial Cloth of Jesus Christ? Garden City, NY: Doubleday, 1978.

Zugibe, Frederick T. The Crucifixion of Jesus: A Forensic Inquiry. New York: M. Evans, 2005.

Zugibe, F. T. "The Man of the Shroud Was Washed." Shroud.com. Accessed 2025.

Popular / Journalistic Sources

Adler, A. D. "An Interview with the Blood Investigator of the Shroud of Turin Research Project." Ancient Origins, 2018.

Catholic News Agency. "Study Claims Shroud of Turin Blood Consistent with Christ's Torture." 2024.

Dowling, M. "The Shroud of Turin: Scientific Testimony to the Suffering and Resurrection of Christ." Matthew Dowling Blog, 2025.

Esposito, Elisa, Roy P. Kerr, and Cosimo Bambi. "Universal Signatures of Singularity-Resolving Physics in Photon Rings of Horizonless Compact Objects." Journal of Cosmology and Astro particle Physics, 2023. https://ui.adsabs.harvard.edu/abs/2023JCAP...01.043E/abstract.

Koinonia House. "A Quantum Hologram of Christ's Resurrection?" Last modified March 31, 2009. https://www.khouse.org/personal_update/articles/2009/quantum-hologram-christs-resurrection.

Magis Center. "The Shroud of Turin and Radiation." September 25, 2024. https://www.magiscenter.com/blog/shroud-turin-radiation-image.

National Center for Biotechnology Information (NCBI). "Image Formation Mechanism on the Shroud of Turin: A Solar Reflex

Hypothesis." November 30, 1997.
https://pubmed.ncbi.nlm.nih.gov/18264452/.

McNair, R. T. J., Dirk Prange, and John Jackson. "Observational Signatures of Hot Spots Orbiting Horizonless Objects." Physical Review D 106, no. 4 (August 11, 2022).
https://link.aps.org/doi/10.1103/PhysRevD.106.044031.

Real Seeker Ministries. "[PDF] Hypothesis for Image Formation on the Shroud of Turin." February 2024.
https://realseekerministries.wordpress.com/wp-content/uploads/2024/02/rucker-paper-34-hypothesis-for-image-formation-on-the-shroud-of-turin.pdf.

Shroud.com. "[PDF] Image Formation and the Shroud of Turin." Accessed 2025. https://www.shroud.com/pdfs/craig.pdf.

Shroud.com. "Testing the Jackson Theory of Image Formation." Accessed 2025. https://www.shroud.com/pdfs/rogers6.pdf.

Shroud3D.com. "Isabel Piczek Article." Accessed 2025. https://shroud3d.com/sculpture-petrus-soons-and-isabel-piczek-theory-resurrection/isabel-piczek-article/.

Shroud3D.com. "Isabel Piczek Article: The Event Horizon of the Shroud of Turin." Last modified 2025.
https://shroud3d.com/sculpture-petrus-soons-and-isabel-piczek-theory-resurrection/isabel-piczek-article/.

Spitzer, R. "Scientific Insights into the Shroud of Turin." Magis Center, 2025.

Up.pt. "Observational Signatures of Hot Spots Orbiting Horizonless Objects." July 23, 2025.
https://sigarra.up.pt/spup/en/pub_geral.pub_view?pi_pub_base_id=626566.

YouTube. "Isabel Piczek - Why the Shroud of Turin Cannot Be a Painting." Published October 14, 2013.
https://www.youtube.com/watch?v=UhaWFFlTpfc.14, 2013.
https://www.youtube.com/watch?v=UhaWFFlTpfc

www.ingramcontent.com/pod-product-compliance
Lightning Source LLC
Chambersburg PA
CBHW020502030426
42337CB00011B/196